# PIERS PLOWMAN

*The Field and the Tower*

*Also by Priscilla Martin*
TROILUS AND CRESSIDA: A Casebook (*editor*)

# PIERS PLOWMAN
# The Field and the Tower

Priscilla Martin

*First published 1979 by*
THE MACMILLAN PRESS LTD
*London and Basingstoke*
*Associated companies in Delhi*
*Dublin Hong Kong Johannesburg Lagos*
*Melbourne New York Singapore Tokyo*

*Typeset in Great Britain by*
*The Pitman Press, Bath*
*and printed in Great Britain*
*by Lowe and Brydone, Thetford*

---

**British Library Cataloguing in Publication Data**

Martin, Priscilla
  Piers Plowman
  1. Langland, William. Piers Plowman
  I. Title
  821'.1   PR2015

  ISBN 0–333–25932–7

TO ABRAM V. MARTIN

# Contents

# Acknowledgements

Chapter 6 is based on my article, 'Conscience: The Frustration of Allegory', which appeared in *Piers Plowman: Critical Approaches*, ed. S. S. Hussey (Methuen & Co. Ltd., 1969). I wish to thank the publishers for their permission to use this material.

I am very grateful for the criticisms and encouragement of these friends and colleagues, who managed not to react like Study even when I was being most like Will: Melvin Buxbaum, Peter Conradi, Janet Cowen, James K. Folsom, Roger Fowler, J. B. Hall, John MacQueen, Paula Neuss, Geoffrey Shepherd.

*August 1978*                                                    P.M.

# Abbreviations

CT  *The Canterbury Tales*. Chaucer, *Works*, ed. F. N. Robinson, 2nd edition (Cambridge, Mass., 1957)

EC  *Essays in Criticism*

ELH  *English Literary History*

JEGP  *Journal of English and Germanic Philology*

MA  *Medium Aevum*

MLN  *Modern Language Notes*

MLR  *Modern Language Review*

MP  *Modern Philology*

PL  *Patrologia Latina*, ed. J. P. Migne (Paris, 1844–55)

PMLA  *Publications of the Modern Language Association of America*

PQ  *Philological Quarterly*

RES  *Review of English Studies*

RP  *Romance Philology*

SP  *Studies in Philology*

# Introduction

*Piers Plowman* is now generally believed to be the work of one man, William Langland, who spent 20 years or more writing and revising his poem.[1] It exists in three major versions, known as A, B and C, and is thought to have been composed in that order.

If we accept, as I do, the theory of single authorship and this sequence of texts, B and C show a process of expansion, local revision of detail and general re-thinking of content. B is about three times as long as A: it provides not only a re-written version of the earlier poem but also a substantial and difficult continuation of it. C expands B, though not to the same extent that B expanded A: it appears to aim at greater clarity through a fuller exposition, as well as re-organising some of B's material and reconsidering B's argument. C shows a tendency to re-write what B had already re-written, as if there were some passages with which the author was never satisfied. The last two passus of C were apparently left unrevised: at least, in all surviving C mss they are essentially the same as those of the B text. Perhaps the completion of C was prevented by the poet's death.

If *Piers Plowman* is by one man, he was obsessively absorbed in it for much of his adult life. He also evidently suffered prolonged dissatisfaction with it. This is suggested not only by the existence of the three versions but also by the conduct of the argument within each text. The poem has a compulsive quality which makes it at once urgent and inept, as though the importance of its religious and moral concerns

1

overwhelmed the poet. Its strengths and weaknesses, its passion and its incoherence, seem closely bound together. Most readers react decisively for or against *Piers*. Those who are captivated by it, as I was, have a tendency to claim its faults as rough virtues. This kind of defence may be moral or aesthetic: in either case it is critically dubious. The exasperating features of the poem – its obscurity, the waywardness of its logic, its obsessional nagging at favourite satirical targets, its digressiveness – move me as evidence of the author's earnestness and sincerity. Yet, while they might be imputed to him for righteousness, it is difficult to see how they constitute literary merit. Unless – a view I also hold but find hard consistently to justify – they are vividly mimetic, mirroring the circuitous and associative qualities of actual thought. This is a less naïve explanation of the poem's strange effects of chaotic authenticity but it is finally open to the same objection. How is one to distinguish between strategic and actual incompetence? Why not praise any sprawling, disorganised, ill-written work for dramatising the experience of intellectual struggle? When the poet confides 'This lokynge on lewed preestes haþ doon me lepe from pouerte' (XI 318), why be charmed by the admission that he is changing hobby-horses in midstream?

Nevertheless, I am affected, reading *Piers Plowman*, by the sense of contact across a gap of six centuries with a mind wrestling with religious, ethical and aesthetic problems which do not admit of direct expression or easy solution. The difficulty of the poem seems to stem fairly from the poet's difficulty in doing something difficult. In one sense any religious poet sets himself a task he considers impossible – to speak in human, inadequate, accommodated language of the inexpressible and incomprehensible – and some of Langland's opacity is consistent with theological explanation.[2] But I suppose this is only one of the reasons why Langland found his project intractable. I suggest that he felt uneasy about his subject in other ways, about poetry itself and his calling as a poet, and about his chosen dominant mode, allegory.

The poet's anxieties seem to be conveyed most directly through the presentation of Will, his narrator, the dreamer of the vision concerning Piers Plowman. All three texts open on Malvern Hills, where Will, dressed as a hermit, is roaming in search of 'wonders'. He falls asleep and has two dreams from which he awakes to Malvern and his poverty and about which he ponders many times afterwards. Here the first section of the poem, the *Visio*, ends. The second part, the *Vita*, tells of Will's search for the states of life called Dowel, Dobet and Dobest. A's *Vita* is very short compared with those of B and C. It consists of one dream and terminates abruptly, a makeshift conclusion reporting Will's death being added by John But. B and C increase the number of dreams and considerably extend this part of the poem.

We are given little direct information about Will in the *Visio*. The opening tells us that he is, is like, or is posing as a hermit and that he is wandering in search of marvels. A vague introduction. Within the dream gadabout hermits are criticised: is Will one of them, censorious of his own faults in others, although honest enough to admit it? In the first vision the information given by Holy Church is largely prompted by Will's questions: do they spring from spiritual earnestness or idle curiosity? Holy Church speaks sharply to him and perhaps hints that his enquiring disposition is merely frivolous and impatient when she says 'This I trowe be truþe; who kan teche þee bettre,/Loke þow suffre hym to seye and siþen lere it after' (I 145–6). Yet, when Will awakes at the end of the *Visio*, he does give prolonged consideration to his dreams and their meaning and validity.

Will's personality emerges more clearly in the *Vita* and is subjected to more overt criticism. His passion to achieve spiritual understanding, the driving force of the poem, is queried and suspected. It may be a form of pride, a version of the original sin of lust for forbidden knowledge. Perhaps Dowel, Dobet and Dobest are merely an intellectual chimaera: the good life cannot be learned, only enacted. Ambiguous itself, the narrator's zeal generates further ambiguities. Will is no respecter of persons: is his intolerance pharisaical or the sign of unworldly rectitude? Does his lack of deference for rank argue purity or uncouthness? Because of it, he tells us, 'That folk helden me a fool' (XV 10), yet he himself accepts the description and speaks often of his folly. He seems to grow increasingly deranged throughout the poem: 'witlees nerhande' (XIII 1); 'And so my wit weex and wanyed til I a fool weere' (XV 3); 'And yede forþ as an ydiote' (XVI 170); 'Wolleward and weetshoed wente I forþ after/As a recchelees renk þat reccheþ of no wo' (XVIII 1–2). Is he merely foolish, the 'doted daffe' (I 140) of Holy Church's rebuke? Is he the traditional wise fool, exploiting his licence as idiot or entertainer to present otherwise unacceptable truths? And is he finally among God's fools in the last passus, who alone refuse to welcome Anti-Christ and, rejecting worldly values, prefer to die than to live? Will's poverty is also emphasised and also vexing. When he wakes at the end of the *Visio*, 'Metelees and moneilees on Maluerne hul-les./Musynge on þis metels' (VII 147–8), does he choose spiritual rather than material wealth and embrace the Christian ideal of poverty? Or is there something indolent and irresponsible in his detachment from the world's work? What, anyway, is Will's occupation? In the B and C *Vita* the waking scene shifts from Malvern to London. Will lives in a 'cote' in Cornhill (C VI 1–2) with his wife and daughter. In A there is a suggestion, deleted in B and C, that he is a minstrel (A I 137–8). In B and C he appears to be a clerk in minor orders, who earns a meagre living hired to say prayers for others on an itinerary around London.[3] In Passus VI of C Reason and Conscience interrogate the Dreamer on whether he actually does anything that can be considered work. Throughout the poem there is debate and discomfort about the position of minstrels and beggars: minstrels may not be useful, beggars may be beyond excuse, and Will's way of life may have something in common with both.

Is Will the Dreamer a self-portrait of William Langland and the poem a kind of spiritual autobiography? He has the same Christian name as the author,[4] is a poet, and is represented as writing a poem on the subject of Dowel, Dobet and Dobest (XII 16–29). In A he appears as a recorder of the action of the poem: the merchants, rejoicing at their share in Piers's pardon, 'ȝaf wille for his writyng wollene clothis,/For he copiede þus here clause þei couden hym gret mede' (A VIII 43–4). George Kane suggests that the poet's use of the name 'Will' at different points in the three texts is a form of 'signature' which evolves with the poem.[5] In A his identity is not made clear until the merchants receive their pardon in Passus VIII. In C, perhaps because the poem and its author had become more widely known, it is manifest almost at once: 'A loueliche lady ... calde me by name,/And seide, "wille, slepest þow?"' (C II 3–5). John But writes of Will as both the character within and the author of the poem: 'Wille þurgh inwit wiste wel þe soþe,/Þat þis speche was spedelich, and sped him wel faste,/ And wrouȝthe þat here is wryten . . .' (A XII 99–101).

Another view is that the Dreamer is an allegorical character, representing the aspect of the human psyche known as the will.[6] There is certainly some word play on this meaning of his name. Thought introduces him thus: 'Wher dowel and dobet and dobest ben in londe/ Here is wil wolde wite if wit koude hym teche . . .' (VIII 128–9). Here the alliteration of 'wil', 'wolde', 'wite' and 'wit', the emphasis given to the nominals by the use of their respective source verbs, the parallel position of the two subjects in the two half-line clauses call attention to the allegorical relationship of the two characters, the interdependence of the two faculties. The will, fallen yet desirous of good, cannot know what is right without the help of the intelligence.[7] Here the opponents of the autobiographical theory would place the emphasis not on the wilfulness of the author but on the wilfulness of Everyman.

The two interpretations are not, in my view, incompatible. The first occurrence of the name in A is open to either reading: the sermon of Conscience and the stirring of Repentance 'made wil to wepe watir wiþ his eiȝen' (A V 44). An allegorical Will fits easily into a scene whose *dramatis personae* include Conscience, Repentance and the Seven Deadly Sins. Literally, reform is impossible until the will is moved by penitence. Reduced to its *sentence* the passage would yield the same meaning if we assume Will to be the author of the poem. But, read thus, I find it more affecting. The direct presence of the author invests the theological commonplace with poignant immediacy. Elsewhere Will shows himself being rebuked by characters within his own poem. The allegorical scheme is consistent enough: the will needs to be controlled and directed by other qualities. If the poet specifically refers to himself, he adds, though perhaps with some violence to the allegory, another dimension of meaning. Instead of being a god-like creator, in control of his work, the author reduces himself to a humiliated creature within it. Rather than possessing quasi-divine foreknowledge of its outcome, he is (or seems) uncertain of how it will unfold. A curious moral intensity is generated by this assault on aesthetic boundaries. If the classic problem of the religious poet is that he confesses his donnée impossible, the didactic Christian writer may also be open to the charge of failing in humility. If we take Langland's Will as both author and *voluntas*, the awkwardness and ambiguity of his presentation are oddly disarming. Will is fallible and the will is fallible. Langland turns to advantage the identity of name and oscillation of meaning: he is enabled to speak directly to his audience, even of self-doubt and self-condemnation, and to exploit the possibilities of a spokesman who is, in an unusually precise sense, a limited narrator.

Will is not the only poet-*persona* in medieval literature who both is and is not the author. The most obvious comparison is with the ironic self-presentations of Chaucer. Yet the name 'Geoffrey' does not, like 'Will', lend itself to multiple significance. A poet with a name which did would be well aware of it, particularly at a time when argument from etymology was often used.[8] This was certainly the case with another poet called Will. Shakespeare makes grim use of the ambiguities of the name in the Sonnets, another work where many readers feel, however unverifiably, the stress and perplexity of autobiographical experience.[9] Shakespeare uses the word 'will' more in its sexual than its theological sense. Yet this produces an effect similar to that of Langland's punning with his name: it evokes the humiliation of seeing oneself as object. Here, too, the author seems to address his audience directly, when he writes of himself as poet, of shame at his way of life, and of the experience of writing these particular poems.

When a poem discusses moral, emotional or aesthetic problems involved in its own composition, I find it difficult to believe that the poet is presenting the anxieties of a fictional character. Sincerity is a slippery concept. Trigorin is a fictional creation, yet his description of the writer's consciousness is probably close to Chekhov's own experience. Conversely, if Shakespeare's Sonnets are autobiographical, they bear witness to the importance of role-playing in the imaginative life. The presentation of the self as both general and particular enables Will to co-exist or to contrast with both the literal and allegorical levels of the poem. Yet at times the particularity of his condition is considered with a seriousness which leads me to think it autobiographical. Will especially impresses me as self-questioning poet rather than fictitious *persona* in the conversations with Imaginatif in B and with Reason and Conscience in C, when he is questioned about the state of his soul and the value of his work. If, however, we took Will to be as fictional as Trigorin, the dialogues might lose some immediacy but would still tell us what anxieties Langland thought natural to the writer of a poem such as his own.

To Langland the state of the writer's soul and the value of his work are aspects of the same question. The question, 'What is the poem for?', points to both author and audience. It asks in what way *Piers* justifies the time and energy spent on its composition, whether it has drained the writer's attention from more important activities and how it can be profitable to others. These issues are all raised by Imaginatif in B Passus XII. This passage occurs near the beginning of B's continuation of the A *Vita*. A possible biographical inference is that the poet is considering his motives for resuming a work he had given up. Imaginatif urges the Dreamer to think of the sinfulness of his condition, the passing of the years and the approach of death. He should amend his life while there is time. Instead, he writes poetry:

> And þow medlest þee wiþ makynges and my3test go sey þi sauter,
> And bidde for hem þat 3yueþ þee breed, for þer are bokes ynowe
> To telle men what dowel is, dobet and dobest boþe,
> And prechours to preuen what it is of many a peire freres.
> XII 16–19

Imaginatif sees the poem as a distraction, something to 'medle with', rather than a proper object for dedication. Will would be better employed in prayer. The poem is not useful: there are already enough books which define Dowel and friars who preach of it. This juxtaposition suggests that

Imaginatif has in mind devotional and theological works. Will's poem seems to him both a time-wasting attempt to set out what is already known and the wrong vehicle for such information. Its only value could be didactic and that need is already met by other books and forms of instruction. Imaginatif does not allow that there might be functions peculiarly well served by poetry. And it does not occur to Will to make this rejoinder. He agrees with Imaginatif and justifies poetry merely as a means of relaxation for the writer:

> I sei3 wel he seide me sooþ, and somwhat me to excuse
> Seide, 'Caton conforted his sone þat, clerk þou3 he were,
> To solacen hym som tyme; so I do whan I make:
> *Interpone tuis interdum gaudia curis.*
> And of holy men I here,' quod I 'how þei ouþerwhile
> In manye places pleyden þe parfiter to ben.'
>
> XII 20–4

Such a defence seems to exclude poetry from the realm of serious communication and enquiry. Its usefulness is private, contributing only to the emotional health of the poet. However, despite Imaginatif's preference for other books and preachers, Will claims that no one seems able to answer his questions:

> Ac if þer were any wight þat wolde me telle
> What were dowel and dobet and dobest at þe laste,
> Wolde I neuere do werk, but wende to holi chirche
> And þere bidde my bedes but whan ich ete or slepe.
>
> XII 25–8

The poem is heuristic, though he would abandon it if he could find the answers elsewhere. He feels a need which nothing satisfies but the poem; he does not claim that only the poem could provide the satisfaction. Rather than seeing a possible justification for poetry here, he becomes defensive about the seriousness of his commitment to virtue. In C this part of the conversation with Imaginatif is omitted. The argument about the moral status of the Dreamer's work occurs in Passus VI, when Reason and Conscience accuse Will of idleness. Here the problem of the value of literature receives even less attention. The emphasis is not on whether poetry is a waste of time compared with prayer but on whether any valid occupation can be discerned in the Dreamer's unstructured style of life. The question 'Is it virtuous to live thus?' has driven out the question 'What does the poem do?'.

According to Imaginatif, what the poem does is describe – unnecessarily – Dowel, Dobet and Dobest. According to Will, it is so far, at Passus XII, an unsuccessful attempt to understand these terms. Imaginatif thinks that the function of *Piers* is to teach but that the work is redundant since other books and teachers 'telle men' the same message. But here Will seems to grope at the possibility that the *author* might learn from his own poem. Langland seems to criticise Will's quest to find Dowel as obtuse, impatient and superfluous. The quest is, nevertheless, an image for the poem. The author does not seem detached from Will's dilemmas, omniscient where his narrator is ignorant. The A text breaks off in mid-dream[10] with Will's violent repudiation of learning; he is obviously in error but the narrator's refusal to continue his enquiry is parallel to the author's inability or reluctance to continue the poem. The B text concludes with the inception of a new quest, as if all that has gone before has proved vain. For structure and metaphor *Piers* draws upon various human activities – pilgrimage, daily work, debate, education – which, however difficult, have clearly defined objectives to be reached by accepted methods. Yet it frequently fails to convey any sense of orderly progression. The search for Truth keeps reformulating itself until it culminates in Piers's mysterious tearing of the pardon. Perhaps the aim of 'finding' Dowel is merely perverse. Piers himself is an elusive symbol of perfection. Will's questions are often left unanswered: possibly they were not even the right questions. Perhaps Langland found his absorption with *Piers* 'busy' in the contemporary pejorative sense, needless anxiety generating further anxiety, his writing and re-writing inimical to doing well. Kynde's final answer, 'Lerne to loue . . . and leef alle opere' (XX 208), is self-evident to the Christian but perhaps it implicitly condemns Langland's passionate commitment to his poem.

It is unlikely that Langland consciously thought of *Piers* as an exploration. Nevertheless, the history of the poem's composition, the degree of re-thinking shown by the three versions and the false starts and changes of direction within each text suggest that this was the poet's experience, if not his theory. Allegory might well be an embarrassing mode in which to conduct an exploration. Often employed for purposes of instruction or propaganda, allegory usually depends upon a received system of ideas. It demands the audience's recognition of its terms or spells out unashamedly what it means. It is particularly successful at analysing – whether in support or revolt – authoritarian doctrines or societies: medieval Christianity, the parallel tyranny of the God of Love, the repressions of Freudian psychology, modern communist totalitarian states. The characters and values in most allegorical works are perspicuous: in *Le Roman de la Rose* and *The Golden Targe*, for example, we know what is represented by Love and by Reason and that Reason should, but probably will not, overcome Love. I suppose that the authors of allegorical works usually begin to write with a clear framework in mind and an end in view.

There are many different kinds of allegory and several are used in *Piers Plowman*. One of the most common is personification allegory, by which an abstraction is embodied in an emblem or actor, such as Patience, Study or the Seven Deadly Sins. The nature of the concepts is analysed when we are shown such personages in action and debate with others. Another means of personification is by the representative character, such as Hawkin who stands for all those engaged in the active life. A different kind of allegorical transference might almost be called depersonification: in XIX Grace equips Piers for ploughing and harrowing with four great oxen called Matthew, Mark, Luke and John and four bullocks, Ambrose, Augustine, Gregory and Jerome. Allegory appears in its sparest form in moralistic nomenclature: in the *Visio* Piers's wife is called 'Dame werch-whan-tyme-is', his daughter 'do-riȝt-so-or-þi-dame-shal-þee-bete' and his son 'Suffre-þi-Souereyns-to-hauen-hir-wille/Deme-hem-noȝt-for-if-þow-doost-þow-shalt-it-deere-abugge/Lat-god-yworþe-wiþ-al-for-so-his-word-techeþ.' (VI 78–82). Piers instructs the pilgrims in an allegorical route to Truth: through Meekness, into Conscience and by

way of various landmarks named after the Ten Commandments. Christ used allegory in the parables and
Langland, like many medieval preachers, follows him in
his use of *exempla*, brief stories which point a moral.
Typology, the study of symbolic relationships between
the events and personages of the Old and new
Testaments, assumes that God gave to human history an
allegorical structure. Langland draws on this tradition
when he re-tells the story of the Good Samaritan: the
two who pass by the robbed and wounded man are
Faith-Abraham and Hope-Moses while the Samaritan is
played by Charity-Christ-Piers.

All these examples may be called allegorical, yet it is
difficult to frame any definition of allegory which would fit
them all. One link between them is that all depend upon a
process of abstraction. It is not true that allegory invariably
makes the abstract concrete. Some kinds of personification
allegory do; even so, a medieval audience might not have felt
Conscience or Holy Church to be pure abstractions. It is not
true of typology, where both terms in the symbolic equation
are deemed to have had historical existence.[11] Yet the
relationship between type and anti-type must be
apprehended at a spiritual level which demands some effort
of abstraction. The names of the members of Piers's family
are intolerable without interpretation: interpreted, they
express the importance for Piers of industry, humility and
patience. The transformation of the Evangelists and the
Doctors of the Church into oxen and bullocks would look as
debasing as the enchantments of Circe, brutification rather
than abstraction, if we were unable to handle concepts of
analogy. Such processes of abstraction begin and end in
theory. *Exempla* preach a general message. Personifications
are meant to speak for all of us. Sustained allegorical works
claim, as naturalistic fiction or confessional poems do not, to
be of universal significance. Allegory is frequently used for
explication. The subjects which are specially hospitable to
allegorical treatment – religion, ethics, psychology, poli-
tics – are those by which we attempt to accommodate our
own experience within a general framework.

Allegory offers considerable advantages for the religious
writer. Through it he can present the inner life as vital and

objective. Its favourite motifs – the journey, the psychomachia, the trial, the debate – are images which insist on the significance of human endeavour. The need to interpret allegory demands earnest attention from the audience; the generality of its claims encourages self-scrutiny. The systematic effect of allegory suggests that the world is morally coherent. But the mode may equally seem limited and facile. For the Christian, the significance of human action cannot finally be judged by human beings. The inner life is largely unknown. The schematic nature of allegory may simplify the problems of moral decision. Its reliance on abstraction may seem a kind of escapism. I do not think it meaningful to make an absolute distinction between allegory and symbolism. But the persistent attempts to do so,[12] the view that allegory is mechanical while symbolism is numinous, evidently stem from dissatisfaction with these aspects of the allegorical mode which may seem more pre-conceived than creative.

My argument is that Langland felt this dissatisfaction, that tensions about his subject and his worthiness to present it were exacerbated by his choice of mode. In such a case problems would compound themselves. The subject, the Christian approach to life, should provide assurance and support; the allegorical mode had always been thought appropriate to it. The difficulties of composition to which A, B and C bear witness might seem almost sinful to their author. The effect of *Piers Plowman* is of strain, of restlessness incongruous with belief. Yet the ways in which it is vexing and exhausting often add to its impact. To say this is not necessarily to claim merit in bad writing. The poem is constructed on a series of dichotomies: between fear and hope, justice and mercy, abstract and concrete, literal and allegorical. The struggle between these forces sometimes results in deadlock or wrenches the poem off course. But the dislocating effects of these oppositions are often functional: through them Langland investigates paradoxes in Christian living which both piety and allegory might evade.

When we accept that the formal unruliness of *Piers Plowman* contributes to its meaning, we are better able to approach one of the major difficulties of the poem. Why, when Langland's theology is orthodox and even optimistic, does his poem convey such a sense of pain and insecurity? Most critics who have written on *Piers* comment on its effects of bitterness and disillusion. Various attempts have been made to explain or explain away the distress of the poem by placing it in the context of contemporary thought and society. Some readers consider it largely a response to the corruption of the fourteenth-century Church. While this is certainly an element in the poem, I think that too much emphasis can be placed upon it. Christians believe that the world is fallen and their faith might as well be strengthened as threatened by evidence of post-lapsarian behaviour. Langland and his contemporaries did not find criticism of the Church on earth subversive of Christianity: when Will expresses doubts about exposing the malpractices of the friars, it is Lewte (Loyalty) who refutes them, insisting that it is a part of Christian duty to be vigilant, out-spoken and uncompromising (XI 85–107). The orthodox view that the unworthiness of an individual did not invalidate his office positively encouraged a critical attitude. Langland, the allegorist, might be able to maintain a steady sense of the absolute value of the Church, while deploring its particular failures in widespread abuses and negligent clergy. Yet his trust in Christian concepts and institutions seems precarious, his narrative and his allegory falter and his poem ends in the climactic anti-climax of Conscience's departure from the Church.

Some scholars have argued that, if *Piers* is placed in the tradition of Christian thought and its orthodoxy is demonstrated, the problems will disappear.[13] It is certainly true that some of the poem's obscurities can be lighted by a knowledge of its theological background. But to know the received body of Christian doctrine is not necessarily to feel it as a support. In the first passus Holy Church descends from the tower to remind Will of her teachings. If they could be fully realised by narrator, audience and poet, the poem might as well end there. But it goes on, to ask questions after the answers have been given, to disappoint our need for pattern and finality, to assert the gulf between field and tower. Allegory, despite its fondness for clear definitions, enclosed gardens and castles, maps, formalities, ethical absolutes, was a mode that went on vexing Langland with problems. My attempt to look at the poem in formal terms will keep bursting out of literary boundaries and bringing me back to the author and his perplexities. Such ways of talking about *Piers* are biographical, intentionalist and suspect: right or wrong, the poem's capacity to provoke them contributes powerfully to its distinctiveness and its impact.

# 1 The Endings

*Piers Plowman*, in all its versions, is divided into two parts known as the *Visio* and the *Vita*. The more detailed organisation of the poem is confusing and perhaps confused, the three texts differ in length and in the relative proportions of *Visio* and *Vita*, but the two-fold structure seems clear. Several broad contrasts between the two parts are also evident: the narrative, for example, is stronger in the *Visio*, the element of debate more prominent in the *Vita*; the characterisation of the Dreamer is more developed in the second part of the poem; the *Vita*, in all texts, is more obscure and digressive than the *Visio*; some questions, particularly those about the value of learning and about predestination, are inherent in the action of the *Visio* but are more explicitly discussed in the *Vita*. In this chapter I shall consider the conclusions of the *Visio* and of the A and B *Vitae* (the end of the C *Vita* having apparently been left unrevised): an attempt to establish their contrasting tones will suggest the central problem we face in interpreting *Piers Plowman*.

The *Visio*, in both A and B, consists of the introduction of Will, two dreams, and Will's waking and reflection upon them. Both visions are concerned with the proper ordering of society and the chances of salvation for individuals and classes in their various occupations. The first dream consists of the panoramic vision of the field full of folk working or idling between the tower and the dungeon, the conversation with Holy Church and the dispute about whether Meed

15

should marry False or Conscience. The second dream opens with the sermon of Conscience (in A) or Reason (in B), which inspires the confessions of the Seven Deadly Sins and the repentance and 'blustering forth' of a multitude of pilgrims to seek Truth. They have no idea how to find the way until Piers, a ploughman, abruptly introduces himself as one who serves Truth and can direct them. He will even guide them to Truth's dwelling himself, provided they will first help with the task of ploughing his half-acre. Piers has considerable troubles with his work force but finally there is a message from Truth.

Although B amends and expands A at many points, the two versions of the *Visio* are similar enough to be considered together for the moment. In the last passus of each a pardon is sent to Piers and his labourers on the half-acre. We are told in some detail the provisions of the pardon, the kind of remission it grants to each class of person and on what terms. Yet, when a priest offers to read it out, it proves to consist of only two lines, the clauses from the Athanasian creed, '*Et qui bona egerunt, ibunt in vitam eternam; qui vero mala, in ignem eternum.*' The priest denies that this is a pardon. It says only 'do wel and haue wel . . . and do yuel and haue yuel' (VI 116–17), and the priest presumably takes this to be a warning of strict justice rather than a promise of mercy. He may have expected the pardon to be a letter of indulgence: when it turns out to be virtually all meaning and no form, he repudiates it. It is clear that he feels the contempt of the 'professional' for Piers and it is equally clear that the author dislikes the priest's professionalism and sides with the inspired amateur. The priest offers to translate Latin for the ploughman but Piers, the type of the simple honest labourer, is miraculously able to answer him in quotations from the Vulgate. Piers tears up the pardon. He announces that he will no longer work so hard, that he will turn to prayer and penance and that the Bible tells us to take no thought for the morrow. The priest and Piers begin to quarrel, each accusing the other of ignorance, and the noise of their dispute awakes the Dreamer.

The *Visio* ends with Will's meditation on this episode. He says that he has pondered it many times. He does not know whether to take dreams seriously: 'Caton and Canonistres'

advise against it; the Bible, on the other hand, tells of
prophetic dreams such as those of Daniel and Joseph (VII
149–72). And what of the pardon? The Dreamer evidently
thinks that the priest has disposed of it, though he perhaps
misreads the priest's hostility to the pardon. The priest,
according to Will, 'preued no pardon to dowel,/And demed
þat dowel indulgences passeþ' (VII 174–5): doing well
requires no pardon; virtuous action will speak more on the
Day of Judgment than letters of indulgence. In this, unless
we take 'indulgences' rather than 'dowel' as the subject of
the second clause, the Dreamer differs from several modern
critics of the poem who see the priest as backing letters of
indulgence rather than virtue and therefore unable to respect
Truth's message. But although the Dreamer appears to
accept the priest's view of the pardon, he is unwilling to
commit himself to any extreme position. He stresses that he
does believe that the Pope has power to grant pardons.
Learned men tell us so and we can find the source of this
doctrine in St. Matthew's Gospel, where Christ says to Peter
'Quodcumque ligaveris super terram, erit ligatum et in caelis: et
quodcumque solveris super terram, erit solutum in caelis: Whatsoever thou shalt bind on earth shall be bound in heaven:
and whatsoever thou shalt loose on earth shall be loosed in
heaven.' (Matt. XVI 19). However, in the Dreamer's opinion, no pardon granted by the Church is as efficacious for
salvation as doing well and he ends the Visio with a prayer
for grace to enable us to do good works and have the support
of 'Dowel' at the Last Judgement.

The tearing of the pardon is one of the most puzzling
episodes in a notoriously difficult poem. It has been variously interpreted. Some readers see the pardon as a statement of the 'eye for an eye' justice of the Old Law which is to
give place to the mercy of the New Law since fallen man
cannot 'do well': the Law would condemn everyone so Piers
renounces it and entrusts himself to grace. The opposite has
also been argued: that a quotation from the Athanasian creed
must suggest the whole context of Christian belief and the
faith and hope it assures. An ingenious compromise respects
both the pardon and the tearing: implying an attack on false
pardons, the actual document gives precious counsel but
must be destroyed lest it be taken for a letter of indulgence.

Yet, as Rosemary Woolf remarks, 'the two theories that in content are most irreconcilable seem truer to the text than the moderate one',[1] as though the enigma of the scene were intrinsic to its power. The tearing of the pardon has been linked with the rending of the veil of the temple at the Crucifixion and with Moses' smashing of the tablets of the Law. Piers's reaction, which should presumably govern ours, is mysterious. Perhaps his anger is with the pardon, perhaps with the priest, perhaps with himself. He may be bitterly disappointed at the terms of the 'pardon'; he may be outraged at the priest's belittling of it; he may be reproaching himself for his concentration on the practical; or he may be indignant that all his hard and honest work has culminated not in a reward but in a command. In throwing himself upon the mercy of God, he may be accepting or rejecting the pardon.[2] Langland himself seems to have found the episode obscure or misleading: he omitted it from the C version.

Piers's violent and baffling gesture is accompanied by a change in his role. The embodiment of honest manual labour announces that he will no longer work so hard. As well as casting himself upon God's mercy, he will rely upon God's power to provide for the morrow. He seems to reject the whole ethic of the *Visio*, its insistence on each man's responsibility to earn his keep in his particular vocation. In Will's inventory of the folk on the field he begins with good ploughmen who 'pleiden ful selde,/In settyng and in sowynge swonken full harde; Wonnen þat þise wastours with glotonye destruyeþ' (Prol. 20–2). Among the evil are the parasites, wastrels, beggars, false religious, those whose superfluity deprives the poor or who live off the toil of others. The vision of Meed deals with questions of just and unjust payment at a fairly theoretical level. The second vision asserts the value of work in the most practical terms. The pilgrimage should not be undertaken until the ploughing is finished. The ploughing stands for all necessary occupations: the knight is obliged not to plough but to defend Christians; poor women should spin and do coarse sewing; noble ladies are to make vestments out of fine materials. The ploughing even makes the pilgrimage redundant, a mere formality compared with everyday duties carried out in a proper spirit. Piers speaks of being Truth's 'pilgrym atte plow' and of how 'my plow-pote shal be my pik' (VI 102–3). Work is prayer. Truth seems to endorse this view in the message he sends with the pardon: stay at home and go on ploughing. Yet Piers turns the metaphor and the meaning inside out when he declares 'Of preires and of penaunce my plou3 shal ben herafter' (VII 124). Prayer is work. As well as the metaphor reversing itself, there is some fluctuation between literal and allegorical levels. The ploughing of the half-acre is the material work of the world which may not be ignored; it also alludes to the parable of the labourers in the vineyard and symbolises all Christian activities. Yet I should feel it an evasion to invoke an allegorical sense of ploughing in order to resolve the contradiction between Truth's advocacy of it and Piers's reservations. As well as destroying Truth's pardon, Piers seems to turn away from his command.

I propose, as far as possible, to consider the last passus of the *Visio* without attempting to ascertain the exact nature of the pardon and the meaning of its destruction. Langland's readers, as well as his characters, are prompted to irritable searchings after Truth, but, so long as we recognise that the pardon does come from Truth,[3] it may be possible to respond to the changing tones of the end of the *Visio* without eliciting a precise message from it.

The last passus of the *Visio* falls into three parts, each with its own distinct atmosphere: the paraphrase of the pardon; the reading of the pardon, the tearing and Piers's dispute with the priest; and Will's awakening and consideration of his dream. The first section, the paraphrase, is leisurely and clearly organised. It proceeds step by step through the classes of society, awarding praise, blame and counsel, so that every kind of person included in it should know exactly where he stands. Even when the content is admonitory, the form of presentation gives a sense of security. The merchants, for example, receive only limited pardon but their response is one of relief and jubilation: 'Thanne were Marchaunt3 murie; manye wepten for ioye/And preiseden Piers þe Plowman þat purchaced þis bulle' (VII 38–9). The Dreamer too considers the pardon reassuring until it is rejected and torn: he speaks later of 'which a pardon Piers hadde þe peple to conforte' (VII 152).

After the controlled and explanatory tone of this account of the contents of the pardon, the revealing of the actual document, in its brevity and intransigence, must be meant to shock. Langland partly achieves this effect by some sleight of hand with his narrative method. The content of the pardon is (apparently) related in all its detail by the Dreamer – in A the grateful merchants reward Will 'for he copiede þus here clause' (A VIII 44) – yet, when the priest offers to translate it for Piers, the narrator reads it over their shoulders and sounds just as surprised as anybody else. 'In two lynes it lay and noȝt a lettre moore' (VII 111): how can all that, the tone implies, derive from just this? Here Langland seems to have reduced an omniscient narrator who knows future as well as past, motive as well as act, to a mere spectator who may grope as much as the reader for the meaning of what he sees. And if the pardon itself astonishes, so does Piers's action in tearing it. I think that this is so, whatever view is taken of the pardon. If we accept the pardon, Piers's destruction of it is shocking. If we reject the pardon, we lose the reassurance which was implied in the paraphrase. And any more complex view can be arrived at only after reflection. R. W. Frank, who proposed the solution that the pardon signifies an attack on pardons, added: 'unfortunately it was a very confusing sign'.[4]

The orderly tone of the paraphrase is followed by the violence of the tearing and the quarrel of Piers with the priest. In contrast with both, the tone of the last part of the *Visio* is anxious and timid as the Dreamer muses on what he has seen. Piers's action in tearing the pardon was spontaneous and confident. He was able to stand up against the representative of the Church and rebuke him in a phrase, 'lewed lorel' (VII 142), which implied that their roles had been reversed. The Dreamer, on the other hand, is hesitant and conventional. Instead of understanding intuitively, like Piers, he worries: 'Many tyme þis metels haþ maked me to studie' (VII 149). When instructions conflict, he has difficulty in making a decision. He cites authorities for and against taking dreams seriously: possibly his decision that dreams are meaningful enough to relate is based not so much on the superiority of the Bible to all other mentors as on a calculation, like Pascal's, that faith involves the lesser risk. On the question of pardons, he believes in all the pardons of St. Peter's Church *and* in the superior efficacy of doing well. While Piers could destroy even a message from Truth, the Dreamer plays safe by clinging to every support he can think of. The nervousness of Will's summing-up makes the reader feel that Piers knew what he was doing. The destructive gesture, even if inscrutable, seems more impressive than the Dreamer's anxious hedging of bets.

A is generally assumed to be an unfinished poem.[5] This assumption (which I share) may have led critics to overlook the ironic relationship between the end of the *Visio* and the end of A's Passus XI. The A *Vita* relates Will's search for Dowel and, after the comparative and superlative terms have been mentioned by Thought, Dobet and Dobest. It consists largely of a series of dialogues with persons or personifications who Will hopes can instruct him: first, in a waking episode, two friars; then, in another dream, the qualities Thought, Wit, Study, Clergy and Scripture. Though eager to learn, the Dreamer is argumentative with his counsellors – understandably, at times, since their instructions are far from lucid. His last conversation, with Scripture, ends in a dispute. When Scripture states that poverty, rather than riches, is conducive to salvation, the Dreamer retorts that, according to the epistle of St. Peter, baptism is sufficient and therefore the baptised rich have the same claim to heaven as the baptised poor. Scripture answers that the text applies only *in extremis*, to those baptised at the moment of death. She alludes to the doctrine that baptism washes away original sin but that, unless he is fortunate enough to die immediately afterwards, the Christian will subsequently commit actual sins. So, despite the gift of baptism, the Christian is also obliged to earn salvation through good works.

At this point the exchange with Scripture breaks off. Possibly the diatribe which concludes Passus XI is addressed directly to her. I do not agree with the suggestion that the Dreamer has woken and, as at the end of the *Visio*, is musing on his dream.[6] He does, however, sound as if he is summing up, even dismissing, all his experience in the *Vita*:

ʒet am I neuere þe ner for nouʒt I haue walkid

To wyte what is dowel witterly in herte,
For howso I werche in þis world, wrong oþer ellis,
I was markid wiþoute mercy, & myn name entrid
In þe legende of lif longe er I were,
Or ellis vnwriten for wykkid as witnessiþ þe gospel:
*Nemo ascendet ad celum nisi qui de celo descendit.*

A XI 258–63

Predestination makes human endeavour meaningless.
Furthermore, God's disposing of salvation seems, by human
standards, unjust. Wise men, such as Solomon and Aristotle, who contributed so much to their successors, are held to
be damned. Evil-doers, however, such as the penitent thief,
Mary Magdalen, King David and St. Paul, the former
persecutor of Christians, are in heaven. These arbitrary
rewards and punishments also raise doubts about the value
of learning: why should we trouble to follow the teachings of
souls in hell, such as Solomon and Aristotle? Their wisdom
did them no good. Nor does he remember that Christ ever
commended learning: on the contrary, Christ promised that
his disciples would be able, through inspiration alone, to
deal with interrogators:

> *Et cum duxerint vos tradentes, nolite praecogitare*
> *quid loquamini; sed quod datum vobis fuerit in*
> *illa hora, id loquimini; non enim vos estis*
> *loquentes, sed Spiritus Sanctus.*

*Mark* XIII 11

But when they shall lead you, and deliver you up, take no
thought beforehand what ye shall speak, neither do ye
premeditate: but whatsoever shall be given you in that
hour, that speak ye: for it is not ye that speak, but the Holy
Ghost.

Learning is worse than useless: it is even dangerous since
intellectuals are more easily led into heresy than the illiter-
ate. The simple faith of the ignorant is the best passport to
heaven:

Arn none raþere yrauisshid fro þe riȝte beleue

Þanne are þise kete clerkis þat conne many bokis,
Ne none sonnere ysauid, ne saddere of conscience,
Þanne pore peple, as plouȝmen, and pastours of bestis,
Souteris & seweris; suche lewide iottis
Percen wiþ a *paternoster* þe paleis of heuene
Wiþoute penaunce at here partyng, into þe heiȝe blisse.

A XI 306–13

This tone is in violent contrast with the conclusion of the *Visio*. The *Visio* ends with the Dreamer's careful statements of faith in the authority of learned men, the efficacy of doing well and the institutional pardons of the Church. The *Vita* ends with desperate fatalism and rejection of the counsel of clergy. It does not matter how one acts, well or badly, since salvation or damnation is pre-ordained; it is useless or perilous to acquire learning. The Dreamer's views are here the opposite of those he held at the end of the *Visio*. His attitudes also stand in an oddly ironic relationship to the behaviour of Piers when he tears the pardon. Like Piers, the Dreamer angrily refuses to concede to the representatives of the Church, but it seems much more ominous to reject the absolute, Clergy (and, on the way, to have vexed Scripture and Study), than to lose your temper with one actual priest and destroy a written material pardon. Abstractions, in this poem, are usually to be treated with more respect than the individuals who try to embody them. Piers fulfils the promise of Christ quoted by the Dreamer: he counters the priest's accusations with inspired wisdom. Will, in contrast, uses the text aridly and negatively. His advocacy of ignorant ploughmen who know only the *Pater Noster* discounts the transformation of Piers into a passionate and 'lettered' disputant. Piers renounces his previous commitment to physical labour but expresses trust in his invocation of Psalm 23. Will's implicit contempt for thought for the morrow is based on despair, on a belief in the malign aspects of providence. The Dreamer's conclusions to *Visio* and *Vita* are suspect in very different ways: the first in its Laodicean orthodoxy; the second in its embittered rejecting heresy. Both contrast with Piers's confidence in tearing the pardon, disobeying the command of Truth and announcing his exodus into a new life.

The errors into which the Dreamer falls at the end of A would be obvious to any educated Christian and, while we may sympathise with his dilemma, we cannot be intended to share it. He not only contradicts the teaching of the Church on actual and original sin, free will and predestination, but commits various *non sequiturs* within his own argument. If, for example, we suppose Solomon and Aristotle to be in hell, this does not necessarily prove their teaching useless. Or, if salvation is pre-ordained and does not depend on the merit of the individual, why not acquire learning? It can scarcely do any harm. Neither, conversely, can the ignorance of the peasant do him any good. Most important, perhaps, the Dreamer ignores, in his discussion of 'unjust' salvation, the fact that all his notorious but redeemed sinners repented and were therefore saved.

Yet it seems probable that the author felt some kinship with his rebellious *persona* at this point: a standard explanation for the abrupt ending of A and its long reworking in B is that Langland gave up because he had reached an impasse in his argument and continued the poem in the B version when he saw ways of resolving his problems.[7] If we accept a partially biographical reading of the poem, B suggests that after the point where A breaks off there was an interval of several years before the poet felt able to resume his work. B XI begins with the account of his surrender to Fortune and his lengthy flirtation with lust of the flesh and lust of the eyes:

> Coueitise-of-ei3es conforted me anoon after
> And folwed me fourty wynter and a fifte moore,
> That of dowel ne dobet no deyntee me þou3te . . .
> By wissynge of þis wench I dide, hir wordes
>     were so swete
> Til I foryede youþe and yarn into Elde.
>
> XI 46–8, 59–60

'Fourty wynter and a fifte moore' need not be taken literally for us to infer from it that there was a long interval between the composition of A and B versions during which the poet to some extent rejected the theological anxieties which had exploded at the end of A. The B Dreamer describes himself

as living in a fool's paradise very different from his scrupu-
lous orthodoxy at the end of the *Visio* or his despair at the
end of A's *Vita*;

> Coueitise of eiȝes ofte me conforted;
> 'Haue no conscience', quod she, 'how þow come to goode;
> Go confesse þee to som frere and shewe hym þi synnes.
> For whiles Fortune is þi frend freres wol þee louye,
> And festne þee in hir Fraternitee and for þe biseke
> To hir Priour prouincial a pardon for to haue,
> And preieh for þee pol by pol if þow be *pecuniosus*.'
>
> XI 52–8

He abandons himself to sensuality, trusting with overt
cynicism to obtain absolution from the mercenary friars.
There could hardly be a clearer back-sliding from the convictions the Dreamer had held at the end of the *Visio* or an
unfounded optimism more different from the end of A's
*Vita*.

I believe that the *Vita* of B is intended as a 'solution' to the
*Vita* of A. This view is supported by B's treatment of the
problems of learning and salvation. A broke off with a dark,
polemical, confused and mistaken view of these subjects.
The Dreamer is engaged with the same questions for most of
the *Dowel* section of the B *Vita*. As in A, he disputes with his
own intellectual faculties and the branches of learning which
might aid him: Thought, Wit, Study, Clergy, Scripture. In B
XI, however, there is a release from this interior debate,
when the Dreamer looks outwards to view from a mountain
the wonders of the earth. This vision is granted by Kynde
(Nature, God as Nature) and contrasts with Fortune's tempt-
ing, narcissistic and illusory vision of Middle Earth shown in
a mirror. After the frustrations and circularities of the
Dreamer's introspection, his contemplation of land and sea,
animals and flowers, seems refreshingly objective. The
argumentative narrator at once sees a flaw in creation: why
does man alone of the creatures appear to lack reason? But
his query is answered in terms other than those in which he
presented it. Will 'reasons with Reason' (XII 218) but Reason
refuses to answer 'reasonably'. Reason, as in *The Phoenix and
the Turtle* 'confounded' by the wonders of metaphysics,

speaks only of the value of suffering and patience. Not all problems can be solved by the exercise of the intellect: some God means to remain mysteries. The Dreamer should take the personal application of this teaching and refrain from being so critical of everyone and everything.

His next interlocutor, Imaginatif, points out that he could have learnt more from Reason, had he not interrupted. The importance of Imaginatif, the faculty of creative reflection and responsible for dreams,[8] also suggests that the poem was abandoned and revised after a lapse of time. Imaginatif introduces himself as one who has never been idle. The aid he will give is predicted in the B revision of Study's speech: storming, as in A, against the penchant of the learned for heretical speculation, she suddenly remarks 'Ymaginatyf herafterward shal answere to youre purpos' (X 119). Like Reason, Imaginatif stresses that one repeats the original sin of Adam by hoping to understand everything. Nevertheless, in Passus XII, he counsels Will on the problems that so infuriated him at the end of A: he demonstrates the value of learning and confronts the problems raised by the theory of limited salvation. Grace is more important than either 'clergy' or 'kynde witte' but learning is to be prized. On it depend the transmission and understanding of the Bible, the celebration of the sacraments, the spiritual help that clerics can give to themselves and to the laity. Sinners can be saved by penitence, as was one of the thieves crucified beside Christ, and it is pointless to take the argument back a stage and ask why that thief, rather than the other, felt penitent: such a question would probe into areas hidden from human understanding. Neither can we know the fate of Socrates or of Solomon but 'God is so good' that Imaginatif is hopeful on the subject of the virtuous unbaptised. We should certainly pray for the heathen philosophers to whom we are so indebted, there are other kinds of baptism without the usual ceremony, and the truth of a good man who lives according to his own law and would believe in a better if he knew it should be rewarded.

While the *Dowel* section of the poem continues to be digressive and perplexing, the vision of the earth and the conversation with Imaginatif are a turning point. Afterwards the Dreamer's enquiries and experience range more widely.

The major characters in the rest of *Dowel* are Conscience, Patience, Hawkin (spotted representative of the active life) and Anima ( whose variety of names suggests a synthesis of all the faculties previously consulted). The Dreamer's interest in these characters evinces a fuller engagement in moral as well as intellectual problems. Will has been temporarily made so docile by Imaginatif as to attend a banquet given by Conscience the more eagerly because Clergy is present. Yet there are further dilemmas and enigmas. Various definitions of Dowel, Dobet and Dobest are proffered, none of them totally clear and conclusive. In the banquet scene Conscience feels obliged to choose between Clergy and Patience. He and Will leave with Patience and meet Hawkin whose multifarious sinfulness casts doubt on whether a good active life, as advocated in the *Visio*, is possible. Will awakes from this dream more distraught than ever: 'And so my wit weex and wanyed til I a fole weere . . .' (XV 3). The next vision opens with the conversation with Anima, the transition from the *Dowel* to the *Dobet* section. Anima attempts to reconcile trust in Providence with human responsibility and speaks largely of Charity but the Dreamer seems sadly unconvinced. He has never met with anyone charitable (XV 152–64) and, after all Anima's exposition, he says 'Ac 3it I am in a weer what charite is to mene' (XVI 3).

There are many guides and mentors in the B *Dowel* but Piers is absent from it. Anima tells the Dreamer that he will not be able to see Charity without the help of Piers, who knows the inner reality behind men's words and works (XV 195–200). As when he tore the pardon, Piers's insight may contradict the apparent meaning of events. But it seems, since we saw him in the *Visio* uncertain how to treat specious beggars and asking advice of Hunger, to have deepened. Anima tells the Dreamer of the Tree of Charity which grows in man's heart, tended by *Liberum Arbitrium* and Piers Plowman. Will swoons for joy at hearing the name and meets Piers again in the second of the two inner dreams. Piers shows him the Tree of Charity and discourses on its symbolic meanings. Will asks for an apple and, as Piers touches the tree, the fruit – great and small, Old Testament patriarchs and prophets, holy men who lived before the Passion – begins to drop and is carried off by the Devil.

Piers, 'for pure tene', as at the tearing of the pardon, throws after him three props, Father, Son and Holy Ghost. The scene shifts abruptly to the Annunciation and the story of Christ's ministry is related. At the Crucifixion Will awakes again into the outer dream. He witnesses the typological drama of the story of the Good Samaritan. It demonstrates that Charity is greater than Faith and Hope and that Abraham and Moses wait to have their revelations completed by Christ, and the souls forfeit to the Devil freed by the Redemption. In the next dream Will finds himself in Jerusalem on Palm Sunday where Christ, looking like the Samaritan and somewhat like Piers Plowman, is to joust on behalf of mankind. This passus, the climax of the B and C *Vitae*, tells the vision of the Christian triumph over evil in the Passion and the Harrowing of Hell. The quarrel between the Daughters of God, standing for mercy and justice, is resolved; the souls in Hell are released. The Dreamer awakes to the sound of the bells of Easter and what he has seen in his vision is re-enacted in the sacrament.

During mass Will falls asleep and dreams that Piers enters 'peynted al blody. . . and riȝt lik in alle lymes to oure lorde Iesu' (XIX 6, 8). He asks Conscience whether this is Piers or Jesus and is told that Christ is wearing the armour of Piers, human nature. Conscience tells Will of the ministry of Christ, relating it to the terms 'Dowel' and 'Dobet', and of the events between the Resurrection and the Ascension. Finally, Christ thought to do best (XIX 182) and gave Piers the power to absolve and forgive. Piers is evidently here a type of St. Peter and the last two passus of the poem, the *Dobest* section, are the subsequent story of the Church. *Dobest*, despite its title, is anti-climactic, a history of failure and compromise. In it we move back to the contemporary world of the Dreamer's lifetime, fourteenth-century English society, the field of the Prologue. The completed B version shows a circularity of thought and structure. *Dobest* has many parallels with the Prologue and first Passus. The beginning and end of the poem show a Church left with the power of St. Peter but ignored or attacked by the forces of worldliness, a society ordered into estates and occupations but open to abuse by kings and commoners, laity and clergy. Verbal motifs are repeated, such as the vital phrase 'as þe world askeþ' (Prologue 19 and XIX 230)[9] and the play on the word 'cardinal' (Prologue 104–9 and XIX 407–23). At the end of the poem Will is still asking questions as he was at the beginning. In my view the parallelism of the opening and close of B is formally satisfying but spiritually distressing. The dream has become a nightmare. The field of folk of the Prologue was not an oppressive place: many people were enjoying themselves even if they should not. The complaint that most men lived only for this world seemed borne out by the gusto of their sharp practices and materialism. They did not see themselves as placed on a dangerous isthmus. The description of society at the end of the poem is far more sinister, its perils shown in images of warfare and espionage, not trade and holiday. While the moralist of the prologue could assign praise and blame with confidence, here corruption is so complete that even Conscience can hardly tell right from wrong. The hordes of Anti-Christ attack the Church; old age, decrepitude and impotence assault the Dreamer. Finally, the Church is infiltrated and Conscience exclaims that he will become a pilgrim and search for Piers Plowman. The Dreamer awakes and the poem ends.

If B was meant to solve the problems left in abeyance at the end of A, it is strange that B's *Vita* should end as desperately as A's, and apparently with more cause for desperation. The whole poem has described a circle back to the world of the prologue. The B continuation seems also to have come full circle. Most Christians are, at the end of B, taking the cynical advice with which Will comforted himself at the beginning: 'Go confesse þee to som frere' (XI 54). A broke off when a fallible narrator rejected Clergy; B closes when Conscience calls in vain for the help of Clergy and abandons the Church itself. In A the Dreamer loses faith in the significance of the actions of the individual; in B we feel the powerlessness of all activities and institutions, of virtues themselves, against the threat of Anti-Christ. Piers has departed and with him the mysterious intuition he showed at the end of the *Visio* and the divine insight that informed him in the *Vita*. The grace bestowed on the Church at Pentecost seems inoperative. The *Visio*, the A *Vita* and the B *Vita* end with three different versions of the desire for salvation: the *Visio* with the 'faithful' destructiveness of Piers who, in contrast to the

Dreamer, can dispense with material proofs and promises; A with the Dreamer's despairing rejection of mercy and free will; B with Conscience finding no safety in the Church and leaving it to become a pilgrim. The quest is one of the organising motifs of *Piers Plowman*. The quest of the *Visio* is replaced by something better: the pilgrimage is delayed for the ploughing; later the ploughing rather than the pilgrimage, is enjoined by Truth; finally, Piers the ploughman declares his vocation to be prayer and penance. In the A *Vita* the Dreamer's quest for Dowel is rejected as pointless. In the B *Vita* a new quest is initiated in the last lines of the poem, to seek Piers Plowman who has disappeared from the ravaged scene of the contemporary Church.

Whitaker, the first nineteenth-century editor of *Piers Plowman*, found the ending 'singularly cold and comfortless'. He complained that 'it leaves the enquirer after a long peregrination still remote from the object of his search, while Anti-Christ remains triumphant and not a single hint is given at the final destruction or the final and universal dominion of his great antagonist'.[10] He even proposed that the poem might be incomplete, in effect reading the abrupt and dark end of *Dobest* as most later critics read the end of the A *Vita*. Its author seems to have felt something analogous in that B, like A, prompted him to a total rewriting of the poem.

While, as far as I know, no later scholar has argued that B is a fragment, most readers find *Piers* a baffling and unsatisfying poem, inconclusive despite the poet's immense labour of revision. Even those who see clarity in the organisation or necessity in the ending feel that the poem expresses strain and disillusion. Yet this effect is difficult to explain in terms of paraphraseable 'content'. Langland voices the central accepted religious views of his time, doctrines believed to console and support. If he diverges at all from total orthodoxy, it is in the direction of greater optimism, in hoping for salvation for everybody. So there is a mysterious discrepancy between argument and atmosphere, between mildness of statement and violence of tone. The stress which recent critics have laid upon the orthodoxy of *Piers* seems to me to emphasise rather than solve the problem.[11]

It may be that the consolations of orthodoxy are overrated. Possibly the paradoxes of Christianity, such as the simultaneous absolutes of God's justice and mercy, must, when deeply felt, produce such tension as I find in *Piers*. Perhaps there is something necessarily inhumane in a religion which places such positive value on suffering. 'Who suffreþ moore þan God?' Reason asks (XI 380), instead of giving the Dreamer a 'reasonable' answer to the problem of evil. On the human level Langland recommends misery, both in self-denial and in the cycle throughout a Christian life of wrong-doing followed by repentance. For example, in B Passus XIV Patience and Conscience examine Hawkin, the active man, and find him more and more spotted with sin. His coat, symbolising his life, is covered with stains and, as he points out, he has only one and does not know what to do about it. After some instruction from the two virtues he is filled with contrition 'and sory gan wexe,/ and wepte water wiþ his eighen and weyled . . . Swouned and sobbed and siked ful ofte . . . and cride mercy faste/, And wepte and wailede and þerwiþ I awakede' (XIV 326–35). Does this dream end sadly or not? Theoretically Hawkin's spiritual condition is more healthy but the stress on weeping and wailing, sobbing and sighing, hardly creates a cheerful tone. And Hawkin is aware that the correct frame of mind will involve permanent suffering, a tension between penitence and the inevitability of sin. It would, he says, have been better to die immediately after baptism 'so hard it is . . . to lyue and to do synne,/ Synne suweþ vs euere . . .' (XIV 325–6). How can he reconcile the command 'Be ye therefore perfect' with the doctrine of human depravity? Some readers have found awkwardness in Langland's allegorical method when the Seven Deadly Sins make their confessions: they object that a 'pure' sin cannot, by definition, regret its sinfulness, repent and mean to change its ways. Yet the immutable nature of these abstractions, the hopelessness of their fumbling resolves to be different, is an extreme version of the case of the living sinful Christian.

It may seem perverse to apply such an anti-Christian argument to an overtly Christian poem. The champions of orthodoxy could reasonably deny that Langland's view of the Christian life is as grim as I have suggested. I have omitted from my account the emphasis on forgiveness, the faith in God's presence and assistance to man. Yet a sense of these consolations often seems to fail in the poem. Piers represents guidance in the *Visio*, redemption in *Dobet*, yet he is absent for long stretches of the *Vita* and is being sought at the end of it. The quality of experience in the poem is not necessarily conveyed or explained by an appeal to the religious beliefs the author affirmed. Langland raises questions in his poem about problems in Christian experience. He knew the 'correct' answers as well as modern literary critics. To supply them as an instant solution to *Piers* may be to by-pass the literary work itself.

The conflict between 'optimism' and 'pessimism', between the argument and the atmosphere of *Piers*, has been reflected in recent discussion of the poem. Whatever their personal religious beliefs, critics have tended to align themselves as orthodox or agnostic readers of *Piers Plowman*. In contrast, however, to the apparently crude, anti-Catholic reading of Crowley's sixteenth-century edition,[12] this has not resulted in ideologically simple Christian and non-Christian approaches. Rather, it has produced critics who see conflict in the poem and critics who deny it. The former argue from their impression of the texture of the poem and the conduct of its argument – an impression of confusion, changes of direction, lack of controlling form – to theological uncertainty and vexation of spirit in the author. The latter claim unity and coherence for the poem, usually by demonstrating that it can be fitted into the Christian schemes of faith and thought of its period. Their strategy of arguing from the intellectual context to the poem often obliges the 'Christians' to display considerable learning but their opponents are likely to question the relevance of the erudition.

Two relatively brief but stimulating essays will serve to illustrate this opposition. In 'Locus of Action in Medieval Narrative'[13] Charles Muscatine attempts to account in formal terms for the tension between statement and feeling in *Piers*. Muscatine argues that a period of 'Gothic' tension in the visual arts, when naturalistic figures or details are seen against a planimetric background, has analogies in literary narrative. Dante is able to exploit two spatial schemes:

Dante's art stands in a typically 'Gothic' poise between

two different systems of seeing, feeling and being. Note, on the one hand, the rationalised pattern, with its numerical hierarchic orderings – reflecting by their locations immutable moral relationships; on the other, the continuously personal and humane response of the pilgrim who traverses this moral landscape, suffusing . . . the abstract pattern with drama and immediacy.

*Piers Plowman*, however, expresses 'Gothic' disintegration:

Langland's space seems surrealistic, unlike the space of any predecessor. For while he knows and in part uses flat, geometric, schematic, Romanesque space; knows and uses in particular scenes naturalistic space; knows and intermittently uses the linear pilgrimage form, none of these becomes a controlling locus of his narrative. The locus of the characters and actions and their spatial environments are continually shifting.

Muscatine connects this phantasmagoric spatial quality with the effects of intensity and strained orthodoxy peculiar to the poem:

Such a formal trait in poetry must have profound consequence for meaning. It almost explains why this, among English medieval poems, is the greatest paradox . . . For while at every turn the discrete isolable episodes – the overt statements – proclaim conservative Christian doctrine, the surrealistic spatial context creates a sense of instability . . . That sense of earnestness, of extraordinary urgency in the poem derives partly from the insecurity of its structure. Unlike Dante's, Langland's fulminations seem not to be issued from under the arching security of a stable, permanent structure. The episodes, fragmentary in relation to one another, suggest shorings, passionately and hastily assembled – from heaven or earth – against some impending ruin.

In *Chaucer and the French Tradition*[14] Muscatine discussed the philosophical implications of style in medieval literature. He argued, with immense influence, that mixed style in

Chaucer, his variety of register, his contrast of high and low conventions, conveys complexity of experience, recognition of both cynicism and idealism, practicality and aspiration. Here he suggests that other aspects of presentation have consequence for meaning. I recognise the 'feel' of the poem in this account and respect its method: in moving from the formal qualities of *Piers* to a description of Langland's religious position, rather than from accepted theology to a scheme of the poem, it is governed by the specific characteristics and peculiarities of its highly individual subject. Muscatine's assertions are not, of course, demonstrable as is, for example, the existence of a patristic gloss on a text quoted by Langland; however, the relevance or the use made of such a gloss is open to question. Muscatine does not invoke context as all-purpose explanation but as another factor in the literary work which requires interpreting. Dante and Langland, in his view, respond to similar spatial possibilities of narrative in opposite ways. They held essentially the same Christian faith, yet it 'works' for one poem and poet as it does not for the other.

Muscatine buttresses his argument by alluding briefly to other unusual formal characteristics of *Piers*:

> The peculiarity of space in *Piers Plowman* cannot alone account for the poem's character. But it works powerfully in concert with such other traits as the periodic establishment and collapse of the dream form, the alternation of allegory and literalism, the violent changes of tone and temper, the peculiar equivalence of concrete and abstract terms, and the indistinctness of the genre.

Although I believe that the areas of literal and allegorical discourse, abstract and concrete vocabulary, can be charted more precisely than Muscatine allows, I find other provoking details of the poem's organisation consistent with his account. For example, in an allegorical poem disagreements between good qualities, such as Study's ill-tempered rebuke of Wit (X 3–12), or Conscience's decision temporarily to remove himself from Clergy (XIII 180–2), suggest either moral perplexity in the author or a desire to shake his audience out of easy certitudes. The suddenness of Piers's

first irruption (V 537) with the news that he knows Truth and
can guide the pilgrims to him implies that help and instruction are both available and deeply mysterious. In the next
chapter I shall discuss in more detail problematic structures
in the poem which I think set 'meaning' at odds with
'message'.

Muscatine finds strain and insecurity in the structure and
atmosphere of *Piers*. By contrast, Elizabeth Salter in *'Piers
Plowman* and the Visual Arts'[15] describes in the poem a world
'concerned only with clarity of exposition', a narrator who
assists us to see it 'in meaningful harmony'. The apparent
shifts of time, location, perspective, subject matter are, *sub
specie aeternitatis*, unimportant; in many cases understanding
of typology will reveal coherent relationships between the
seemingly diverse. Knowledge of the Christian assumptions
and the aesthetic conventions helps us to restore patterns of
meaning in the poem, just as we have to learn to 'read'
medieval painting and drawing. Professor Salter recognises
the need for tact in adducing analogies from the visual arts,
particularly in the case of a poet who seems suspicious of the
allure of beautiful artefacts. She aptly retorts, for example, to
a suggestion[16] that Langland's unlocalised 'empty' settings
are similar to the plain backgrounds of such medieval
paintings as the *Wilton Diptych*: 'The effect of gold leaf, or
gold paint . . . is hardly ever that of "emptiness" . . . it
functions as a spiritual comment . . . It is almost the reverse
of emptiness.'

Yet, as she criticises Muscatine's account of the poem, I
find her own use of analogy unconvincing:

> The only control exercised over the choice, disposition and
> relating of materials is spiritual; it is not so much an
> 'insecurity of structure' that we find *Piers Plowman* as a
> deliberate attempt to work on a principle familiarly
> expressed by Langland's contemporary, the author of *The
> Cloud of Unknowing*: '"Wher then", seist thou, "schal I be?
> Nowhere bi thi tale!" Now trewly thou seist wel: for there
> wolde I have thee. For whi nowhere bodely is everywhere
> goostly . . .' Langland's reluctance to show his reader, or
> his dreamer, any sympathy for that irritable ques-
> tion – 'Where, then . . . am I to be? Nowhere, according

to you!' – is crudely understood as an admission that stability and security are lost. Rather, it is a direction towards a new stability – a coherence to be discovered only fragmentarily in history or fiction, regarded as sequential narratives, but most fully in the great spiritual themes that inform them.

She compares the Dreamer with Bosch's saints in prayer surrounded by 'landscapes fashioned strangely from inner and outer reality', with the Psalmist in the *Utrecht Psalter*, a 'focus of attention' for a work which 'clearly asks to be "read" not as a continuous and self-sufficient narrative, but as an exploration of deeper harmonising truths'. This is surely a perversely generous view of the Dreamer.[17] He himself feels the initial landscape of his dream to be a 'wilderness': if we were to draw an analogy with the *Wilton Diptych*, it is as though the Dreamer were usually confined to the world of the left-hand panel and unable to see the heavenly consolations of the right-hand panel. Unlike a saint in prayer, he interrupts and argues and is accused by Imaginatif of wasting time on writing instead of praying. He is far from the state of advanced contemplation that *The Cloud of Unknowing* discusses. The author of the *Cloud* might well have been suspicious of Will. He saw the possibilities of misusing good counsel, the danger of false states of apparent sanctity. He begins his book on contemplation by forbidding the merely curious to read it. It is not for the kind of spiritual dilettante whom Study sees in Will. Throughout the poem Langland dwells on the subject of wolves in sheep's clothing, on the possibility that apparent prayer may be evasion of work, on the themes of hypocrisy and self-deception. The Dreamer is associated with all these dangers; no one but Piers can distinguish between 'inner and outer reality' (XV 198–200). The poem may well be 'an exploration of deeper harmonising truths', or at least a search for them, but Professor Salter's argument ignores a good deal of disharmony between the narrator and his inner and outer environment.

Undisturbed 'Christian' readers of *Piers* often refer us to context and analogy – Professor Salter to the visual arts,[18] Robertson and Huppé to patristic tradition,[19] Bloomfield to millenialist theory and monastic philosophy[20] – to prove that Langland believed what, by the standards of medieval Christendom, he ought to have believed.[21] Their task is, at one level, an easy one, since he did believe it. The theology of *Piers* is orthodox and indeed optimistic, possibly eccentric only in its generous hope for universal salvation. But to argue from its intellectual context that *Piers* must express harmony and assurance is to ignore the most problematic and individual features of the poem. To me *Piers* conveys frequently – and finally, at the end of each version – a mood of strain and anxiety. I do not think that this makes the poem heterodox in its message and I would not wish to defend my reading by an appeal to social context, to the abuses in fourteenth-century Church and society which might have given grounds for pessimism. The dichotomy between faith and experience, between Christian conviction and personal distress, is conveyed by *Piers* itself through the formal strangeness of the poem's methods. Langland believed in the great medieval theological schemes yet his own narrative and symbolic schemes are persistently unreliable. Debates, pilgrimages, ploughing, pardon, quests, battles against Anti-Christ are proposed as means to knowledge or virtue but end in inconsequence or raise as many problems as they solve. And, since the poem is largely allegorical, the frustrations of the story lead us to question the metaphors through which it proceeds. Langland sometimes sabotages his allegory as well as his narrative and the sabotage itself is part of the poem's meaning.

# 2 Ironic Structures

*Piers Plowman* impresses most readers with a sense of disappointment and frustration. This effect is reported of all versions of the poem, not merely of A with its short *Vita* and abrupt conclusion. Langland did not make one unsatisfactory attempt at *Piers* and then rewrite it in a form which appears final. The A version provoked B, the B version provoked C, and most critics and editors of B and C find the later, fuller poems vexing and unresolved.[1] The A text may be incomplete, the B text complete, yet, as we have seen, they end on similar problems and anxieties. I cannot feel that, even if he had finished C, the author would have rested content. As Mary Carruthers puts it: 'Had the revision of C been completed, there would undoubtedly have been a D – or an E – text, until death or fatigue ended the process arbitrarily.'[2] The work would always be in progress; something intransigent in the poem, something unappeased in the poet, would drive it on indefinitely.

Yet it is difficult to see what, in the argument of the poem, should produce such permanent dissatisfaction. A few 'Christian' critics deny that *Piers* expresses anguish and uncertainty.[3] But most scholars of the poem, from Whitaker on, have found its drift deeply pessimistic. 'I do not think that theology may be invoked to unsay poetry,' writes E. T. Donaldson, claiming that *Piers* expresses, if not 'theological', 'poetic despair'.[4] I would agree with both the description and the distinction. The poetic despair seems at odds with the theological correctness, is perhaps even exacerbated by

38

it. Rather than invoke the disillusioning context of the fourteenth-century Church to explain the distress of *Piers* or the reassuring scheme of Christian orthodoxy to refute it, we should consider in poetic terms how doctrine and despair interact. In his article on 'Locus of Action' Muscatine makes such an attempt: he finds the poem a paradox, proclaiming conservative Christian beliefs, yet conveying, through its spatial peculiarity, its indistinctness of genre, its phantasmagoria of the literal and the allegorical, the abstract and the concrete, a passionate effect of insecurity. In this chapter I shall try to account, in similarly formal terms, for some aspects of this paradox. I shall propose that it is expressed through ironic structures: narrative patterns disrupted in the interest of the argument, ideological statements undercut by poetic and dramatic techniques.

In all versions *Piers* organises itself through schemes which break down, initiates actions that are not completed, asks questions which remain unanswered. All sections and versions of the poem end in frustration and anti-climax: the *Visio* closes, not on the pardon, but on the Dreamer's nervous perplexity about its tearing; the A text leaves Will in despair about the chances of salvation and the significance of striving for it; B ends with the success of the forces of Pride and the flight of Conscience from the Church. Within each version the relationship between the sections gives a sense of back-sliding. In A the faith (however timid) of the end of the *Visio* is succeeded by the despair (however unwarranted) of the end of the *Vita*. In B and C the terms Dowel, Dobet and Dobest seem to propose for the *Vita* an ascending sequence rather than the exalted climax of the Passion and the Harrowing of Hell in *Dobet* followed by the blurring of faith and insight in *Dobest*. *Piers* not once but habitually develops towards conclusions in which nothing is concluded.

The 'indistinctness of genre' contributes to the atmosphere of restlessness and indecision. *Piers* employs, but haphazardly or as if they will not 'work', the forms of dream vision, debate, pilgrimage, encyclopaedic satire, psychomachia. Attempts to categorise the poem are hopeless: it is unlike anything else. But, equally, medievalists use a catalogue of familiar terms before they confess themselves defeated by its strangeness: *Piers* is in many respects like many other Middle English poems but it refuses to stay within the boundaries of any of the conventions it appropriates. These formal structures seem to break under the poem's weight of meaning or the poet's impatience. Perhaps he found them rigid and constricting, traditional accepted forms which inevitably allude to previous achievements made within them. The locations of the poem dissolve or are left vague, personages irrupt unannounced or vanish abruptly. Similarly, the genres are discarded or confused as though trust should not be placed in them. The effect is sometimes of incompetence and failure with form. It is equally of innovation and experiment with form.

Langland is both careful and unceremonious with the narrative conventions he employs. This is most obvious in the structural framework provided by the dream vision. The poem opens with details familiar in this genre: a rural landscape, a May morning, a weary narrator lulled asleep by the sound of a stream. It is a beautiful opening but, by the time he wrote the C text, the poet seems to have been tiring of its conventional elements: he cuts the evocative lines about gazing at and listening to the water and emphasises the narrator's curiosity with the functional: 'Ich . . . sawe meny cellis and selcouthe þynges' (C I 5). In *Le Roman de la Rose*, *Pearl*, *The Golden Targe* and many other poems in this form, the narrator begins to dream of an idealised landscape, inhabited by allegorical creatures and ready to yield spiritual insight. But if the opening lines of A and B suggest that such a dream will follow, the expectation is derided by the rest of the Prologue. Will is at first baffled by the world of his dream:

> Thanne gan I meten a merueillous sweuene,
> That I was in a wildernesse, wiste I neuere where,
>
> Prol. 11–12

but it turns out to be the world of ordinary everyday life in all its confusion and variety and the Prologue ends, as if to assert its verisimilitude, with the street cries of London. The effect is to blur the distinction between sleep and waking. These states are sharply contrasted in other dream poems and Langland's departure from the convention makes us question its truthfulness. Perhaps it is only through the spectacles of habit that waking life appears manageable and well charted: viewed with the objectivity of innocence or vision it might be revealed as a 'wilderness', as illogical and unpredictable as any dream.

Throughout the poem Langland breaches the decorum of the dream form in various ways. Traditionally in such works the waking area is primarily the realm of the literal, the dream of the visionary and allegorical. But in the first dream setting of *Piers Plowman*, the field of folk, literal and allegorical characters, individuals and types, jostle against each other and are even hard to tell apart. Those who 'putten hem to pride' (Prol. 23) or 'chosen chaffare' (Prol. 31) are presented a trifle more abstractly than those who 'putten hem to plouʒ' (Prol. 20) or 'in preieres and penaunce' (Prol. 25). Such slight variations scarcely constitute a change of mode within ten lines. Yet it is symptomatic that these classifications should be slightly awry when they introduce a cast of characters as diverse as, on the one hand, hermits, pilgrims, pardoners, jesters, beggars, friars, parish priests, bishops, cardinals, lawyers, bakers, brewers, butchers, weavers, tailors, tinkers, masons, miners, ditchers and taverners and, on the other, tyrannical cats and angels who bend from the sky to utter monitions in Latin verse. The confessions of the Seven Deadly Sins, though the form is that of a standard allegorical tableau, show a similar fluidity of classification. In B the first Sin is called 'Pernele proud-herte', which might be the name and nickname of an actual proud woman; the second, less individualised, is merely 'Lechour'; the expected sequence of abstractions follows – 'Enuye', 'Wraþe', 'Coueitise', 'Sleuþe', but it is interrupted by 'Gloton'.[5] The same scene includes the hypostatisations Reason, Conscience and Repentance, together with Robert the Robber, either an individual or representative character – it is impossible to say which – who interrupts their general counsel with the sad particularity of his own dilemma. I shall discuss in a later chapter the clash between modes at the dinner given by Conscience, whose guests are the allegorical Clergy and Patience, the Dreamer, and the literal doctor of divinity who may actually be based on a contemporary friar.[6]

The confrontations in such a scene are made possible by Langland's apparent vagueness about the boundaries of the dream form, his unwillingness to demarcate an area of visionary insight purged of the complexities and contingencies of ordinary life.

Within the dreams literal characters co-exist with abstractions. Even more unusually, allegorical characters occur in some of the waking episodes.[7] In Passus XX the appearance of Need to the hungry unhappy Dreamer seems like an hallucination. The effect of displacement increases the ambiguity of his advice. He condones stealing and advocates total poverty. Does his escape from another realm of discourse make his counsel more or less authoritative? Should it demand the same kind of respect as the utterance of a ghost, or should it be scrutinised with literal-minded suspicion as possible delirious fantasy?[8] The literal impact of Will's conversation with Reason and Conscience in C VI is so strong that the passage is known as 'the autobiographical episode'. The abstractions converse, in the waking world of money and Cornhill, with a narrator who looks less like *voluntas* than like the poet himself. Extremes meet: Reason and Conscience, independent of a dream setting, strike me as doubly allegorical; Will, poet as well as character, looks doubly literal.

Langland also experiments in *Piers* with a multiple dream structure, unfolding the narrative through a number of dreams and awakenings. The A text contains three visions, the B text ten and the C text nine.[9] The time span of the outer narrative, the Dreamer's waking experience, is much longer than in other dream poems. In it the scene shifts from Malvern to London and Will wanders, makes his poems, dallies with 'Coueitise-of-eiȝes' for 45 years, changes in appearance, grows old and impotent. In contrast with other poems in the same genre *Piers* yields its revelations in a gradual, fragmentary and progressive way. The narrator of *Pearl* learns, the narrator of *The Parliament of Fowls* fails to learn, from one vision. But Will's dreams and his reactions to them dramatise the insights, meditations, perplexities, impatience, development, fatigue of a whole lifetime. Langland even risks some narrative ineptitude to stress the plurality of the visions. The second dream is introduced thus:

> Thanne waked I of my wynkyng and wo was withalle
> That I ne hadde slept sadder and yseiȝen moore.
> Ac er I hadde faren a furlong feyntise me hente,
> That I ne myȝte ferþer a foot for defaute of slepynge.
> I sat softely adoun and seide my bileue,
> And so I bablede on my bedes, þei brouȝte me aslepe.
> Thanne mette me muche moore þan I bifore tolde . . .
>
> V 3–9

There is no pretence at probability here: Will wakes and is promptly overcome with exhaustion through lack of sleep; it is clear that he wakes only to fall asleep again so that there shall be a *second* dream.

There are not only a number of consecutive dreams in *Piers* but also two dreams within dreams, turning points in the advance of Will's understanding. Each provides a new allegorical dimension in the poem. The first occurs (XI 5–406) during the argument with Scripture about salvation with which A broke off. In it Fortune shows the Dreamer his own life in a mirror, Trajan appears to bear witness that he has been saved and Kynde reveals the wonders of Middle Earth. In the second inner dream (XVI 20–167), Piers re-enters the poem after his long absence from the B *Vita* and shows Will the Tree of Charity. There follows a vision of the life of Christ, from which Will awakes not to the scene of the outer dream, his conversation with Anima, but to the meeting with Faith. These inner dreams are allegories within allegories yet both culminate in a vision of the literal, the actual creatures of Middle Earth, the historical life of Christ,[10] including in the scope of their revelation all human space and time.

The purpose of the number of dreams and of the inner dreams seems obvious upon reflection. But they are features of the poem which can look, on a first reading, arbitrary and uncontrolled. If a delayed effect of the sequence of visions is of progressive revelation and understanding, the immediate impression is of incompleteness and interruption. Will wakes at the beginning of Passus V in order to fall asleep again. Equally, he wakes in order to be disappointed

'Thanne waked I of my wynkyng and wo was withalle,/ That I ne hadde slept sadder and yseiȝen moore' (V 3–4). This note of chagrin and frustration is struck after several of the visions: '[I] awaked þer-wiþ; wo was me þanne/That I in metels ne myȝte moore haue yknowen' (XI 406–7); 'Ac after my wakynge it was wonder longe, Er I koude kyndely knowe what was dowel' (XV 1–2); 'Thanne as I wente by þe wey, whan I was thus awaked,/Heuy-chered I yede and elenge in herte' (XX 1–2). The structure of Piers suggests that no gain is permanent, no understanding final. The awakening in the last line is, by implication, the most bitter of all. The triumph of Christ in Dobet and the gift of grace to the Church seem inoperative as Conscience struggles in vain against the enemy and leaves to search for Piers Plowman. And whatever Will has learnt is dismissed: it is shrugged off in the line 'He lyþ adreynt and dremeþ . . . and so do manye oþere' (XX 377), as if the whole form of the poem were being attacked.

As an organising structure in the poem, the dream sequence both clarifies and confuses. The treatment of the terms Dowel, Dobet, and Dobest is yet more vexing. The Dreamer, searching for spiritual enlightenment, enquires about Dowel and is told also of its comparative and superlative. The Vita uses the three terms as a general title and the individual terms to mark stages in the poem. This might, elsewhere in medieval religious literature, be a means of elucidating the subject and furthering understanding: the conscientious logic of definition, division and sub-division was thought relevant and helpful to the most inward spiritual experience. The Scala Perfectionis, for example, opens with advice on the relationship between the inner and outward lives of the Christian, discussion of the active and contemplative vocations and an account of the three degrees of contemplation, subdividing the second degree and explaining the difference between the second and third. This method of exposition, like the ladder image of the title, suggests that the Christian life can be an orderly and well-charted progress.

In Piers, however, the method is merely exasperating. The Dreamer asks Thought about Dowel, which he already finds sufficiently elusive (VIII 76–7): Thought's reply casually generates two more desiderata so inimical to definition that

'Dowel and dobet and dobest þe þridde' has been described by one critic as nothing more than a 'maddening refrain'.[11] The terms are continually discussed in the *Vita* but no explanation ever seems conclusive. Even our sense that the comparative and superlative must be a progression is sometimes jolted: in A Wit appears to advise one who does well against striving to do better (A X 88–9); Thought suggests that Dowel and Dobet could act against Dobest and be punished (VIII 100–6). Attempts to pin down the terms and assign precise meanings to them seem perverse. Their meaning is either so profound that it cannot be conveyed by periphrasis or so obvious that explanation is redundant. Thought says that these virtues 'ben noȝt fer to fynde' (VIII 79); Wit tells Will that 'Sire Dowel dwelleþ . . . noȝt a day hennes' (IX 1); Imaginatif thinks the poem a waste of time when there are already plenty of books and preachers to tell people what Dowel, Dobet and Dobest are (XII 17–19). Yet Will protests that he does not understand and that he can find nobody to explain them to him (XII 25–8).

The problem can be seen as stemming from Will's personality. Throughout the poem his interlocutors accuse him of being theoretical and impatient in his search for understanding. Before 'Dowel' has ever been mentioned, Holy Church hints at Will's propensity to stand in his own light: 'This I trowe be truþe; who can teche þe bettre,/Loke þow suffre hym to sey and siþen lere it after' (I 145–6). Study's diatribe against those who misuse knowledge ends with another implied criticism:

And þo þat vseþ þise hauylons for to blende mennes wittes,
What is dowel fro dobet, now deef mote he worþe,
Siþþe he wilneþ to wite whiche þei ben alle.
But he lyue in þe leeste degre þat longeþ to dowel
I dar ben his bolde borgh þat dobet wole he neuere,
Theiȝ dobest drawe on hym day after ooþer.

                                                            X 134–9

One cannot 'learn Dowel' by going on a quest to find where 'he' lives, by asking others to give lectures on the subject, least of all by trying to distinguish intellectually between

Dowel, Dobet and Dobest: Will, who has reversed the sequence of action and understanding, should do well rather than create difficulties for himself.

Another aspect of the trouble is that Will bases his enquiry on a false structure. Earlier critics of the poem were inclined to follow him in searching for definitions of the 'three lives'.[12] Several recent studies, however, have pointed out that Will sets a grammatical trap for himself.[13] He takes 'do wel', an imperative, as a noun, treats it as an actual person and goes to look for it as though it were one discrete entity. Compounding confusion – or highlighting it – Thought produces a comparative and superlative, forms which nouns do not have, so that Will goes in quest of not one but three incomprehensibles. The perversity of the attempt is underlined by the grammatical ineptness of 'dowel' in almost every context in which it occurs. The awkwardness of the collocation 'Do well is' should warn one against trying to complete the sentence. Imperatives ask for action, not for re-formulation. Nor is any one activity the only correct response to the command to do well. In the dinner scene Clergy confesses himself unable to define the terms since Piers has 'impugned' the sciences 'and demeþ þat dowel and dobet arn two Infinites,/Whiche Infinites, with a feiþ, fynden out dobest' (XIII 124, 128–9). 'Infinites' are, presumably, not susceptible to definition. Yet it is characteristic of *Piers* to tantalise the reader with the appearance of an organisation which it rejects as inadequate to experience.

Anne Middleton opens a valuable article[14] on 'infinites' by pointing out that the word has two meanings which are virtually opposed to each other. 'Infinite' can mean 'lacking boundaries, formal limits, incomplete' or 'all-inclusive, self-defining, perfect'. She convincingly claims that the relevant meaning in XIII 128–9 is 'imperfect' rather than 'perfect'. Yet, as she remarks, Langland's choice of the term creates the largest possible area for misunderstanding: 'It is . . . utterly characteristic of Langland to choose a word whose range of possible meanings contains the paradox that his use of the term seems to resolve'. She points out that 'infinite' was used by medieval grammarians in connection with two parts of speech, the uninflected verb and the interrogative pronoun. The infinitive (often found in sentences expressing volition or command) was thought of as incomplete; in *Piers* we might say that the infinite governs an indefinite number of occurrences of the finite verb, particular actions at particular times. The pronoun *quis* is infinite in that referent is unknown to the speaker: it seeks a finite knowable substance in answer. In so far as the terms are allegorical they ask for understanding of abstract relationships rather than one-for-one substitution of other terms. This abstractness, Anne Middleton argues, is functional: 'By drawing his complex metaphor from the realm of intellectual rather than sensory reality, Langland has created in his triad an explanatory instrument which is as free as is poetically possible from the merely contingent.' Will therefore mistakes question for answer, abstract for concrete, actions for states, the incomplete for the complete. Yet his premises are never directly challenged: we are forced to share with him the frustration of trying to conduct an argument based on a logical error.

It is characteristic of *Piers* that one of the submerged references in the mysterious 'infinites' should be to the interrogative pronoun. There are many exchanges of question and answer in the poem. Some of them, however, are scarcely informative. Some answers, such as Thought's on Dowel, compound rather than solve a problem. Some of the Dreamer's questions provoke further questions from the reader. Within the poem his allegorical mentors sometimes complain that his queries are redundant, that he knows the answers already. He seems at times to fall almost compulsively into the interrogatory vein:

> 'What art þow', quod I þo, 'þat my name knowest?'
> 'Þat þow woost wel', quod he, 'and no wiȝt bettre.'
> 'Woot I?' quod I; 'who art þow?' 'Þouȝt', seide he þanne.
> 'I haue sued þee seuen yeer; seye þow me no raþer?'
> 'Artow þouȝt?' quod I þoo . . .
>
> VIII 72–6

The banal repetitions of ordinary conversation survive in the visionary dialogue, along with a tone of earnest stubbornness as Will twice asks Thought questions which he has just answered. His enquiries both propel and retard communication, he both courts and resists instruction. Question-answer enthrals Will so much as a structure that he is capable of reversing the sequence or re-playing passages in a series.

In Will's first conversation in the poem with Holy Church all his questions, after the initial 'what may þis bymeene?' (I 11), are themselves questionable. Despite his eagerness to be instructed, Holy Church becomes exasperated with him. She thinks him wilfully ignorant, demanding information that he should already possess. He ought already to know who she is (I 75), he has been given 'kynde knowyng' of natural law (I 142), he should receive teaching patiently and learn from it (I 146). Some of Will's enquiries are puzzling because of a vague openness, so that one does not know what sort of answer they should receive or even whether they were reasonable questions. For example, when Holy Church counsels moderation in use of food and drink, the Dreamer asks 'Ac þe moneie on þis molde þat men so faste holdeþ,/ Tel me to whom þat tresour appendeþ' (I 44–5). Is this a naïve question, as if Will supposed that money had only one constant owner? Is it a subversive one, anticipating the envious friars of the last passus who believe that all should be held in common? Or does it implicitly criticise as simplistic the advice of Holy Church who merely advocates self-control and ignores economic problems of the relations between work, status, payment and prices? Holy Church thinks the Dreamer a 'doted daffe' (I 140) but one critic has found him 'Swiftian'.[15] After Holy Church has told him about Truth, she makes to depart. Will, however, detains her and asks to know about the False. Is this an example of perverse curiosity, linking the Dreamer's desire for knowledge with the original sin of Adam?[16] Or does it, in its care to establish the boundaries of the term, seek to define Truth by its opposite and conform to the logical methods of medieval enquiry?[17] Or does it, like the unwelcome comparative and superlative of Dowel, propose a semblance of orderly method which might turn out to be a false structure?

From Will's interrogation of Holy Church to his final imploring 'Counseille me, kynde, . . . what craft is best to lerne?' (XX 207) the poem is full of questions. The enquiring tone is not confined to the narrator: the King in the first vision adopts it with Reason, the pilgrims with Piers, Hawkin with Patience and Conscience. The debate, an extended version of question and answer, statement and refutation, also occurs several times: the contest between Conscience and Meed, the presentation of Peace's case against Wrong, the argument of the daughters of God, even the confrontation of Christ and Satan at the Harrowing of Hell, take this form. Through it some truths prevail: Conscience, even if he cannot finally disarm Meed, does expose her nature; Christ resolves the daughters of God, the claims of his justice and mercy, into harmony. But in the hands of the Dreamer the method is usually fruitless. The whole of the A *Vita* and much of the B and C *Dowel* consist of debates initiated by Will which generally have the ironic effect of leaving him further from enlightenment than ever.

The *Vita* opens with an encounter with two friars whom the Dreamer asks about Dowel. He greets them courteously – 'I hailsed hem hendely as I hadde ylerned/And preide hem *pur charite* . . . If þei knewe any contree . . . Where þat dowel dwelleþ' (VIII 10–13) – but swiftly becomes argumentative at their claim that Dowel lives with them: '"*Contra!*" quod I as a clerc and comsed to disputen . . .' (VIII 20). If, as the Bible says, even the righteous man sins seven times a day, Dowel cannot always be present among the friars. Their reply, a distinction between avoidable venial sin and destructive mortal sin, has been criticised but more often accepted;[18] if valid, as I think it, the exchange dramatises the self-inflicted frustrations of the Dreamer's conduct of his quest for Dowel. Will looks more interested in scoring off the friars, both as rival intellectuals and as members of an order compromised by scandal, than in learning from them about doing well.

Will then falls asleep and dreams of conversations with allegorical characters such as Thought, Wit, Study, Clergy, Scripture. The teaching of the friars may have been open to question. But when the investigation continues at the deeper allegorical level the counsel of the abstractions, while it may be limited and dramatic, is surely to be trusted. Yet the Dreamer is just as rebellious with them as he was with the literal characters. He was briefly courteous to the friars but soon became disputatious. Their smugness may have been provoking but his encounters with the essences of wisdom and learning themselves follow the same pattern. Study's anger with frivolity and irresponsible controversy reduces Will to 'mekenesse' and 'mylde speche' (X 152):

> And whan I was war of his [Wit's] wille to his wif gan I knele
> And seide, 'mercy, madame; youre man shal I worþe,
> As longe as I lyue, boþe late and raþe,
> For to werche youre wille while my lif dureþ . . .'
>
> X 147–50

Responding to his humility, Study directs him to Scripture and Clergy but he is soon quarrelling with them in the same tone that he used to the friars: '"*Contra!*" quod I, "bi crist! þat kan I wiþseye/And preuen it by þe pistel þat Peter is nempned . . ."' (X 349–50). He has no qualms at competing with Scripture and Clergy in logic, theology and knowledge of the Bible. The debates of medieval literature can be generally divided into 'horizontal' and 'vertical'. The horizontal debate, as in *Winner and Waster*, *The Owl and the Nightingale*, *The Parliament of Fowls*, is between evenly matched speakers, where each tries to win support for his view but none is conclusively victorious. The vertical debate, as in *The Divine Comedy* or *Pearl* between characters unequal in understanding, shows the inferior profiting, despite emotional and intellectual handicaps, from the counsel of the superior. We can account in formal terms for the frustrating effect of the Dreamer's enquiries about Dowel: as well as mistaking the nature of the subject, he keeps turning a vertical debate into a horizontal one. In this interior drama the *peripeteia* is not of action but of thought.

Unanswered questions and incompleted actions are characteristic of *Piers Plowman*. Will interrupts, delays the argument, gives up in despair, creates misleading structures for his enquiry but the dislocations in the narrative cannot all be ascribed to the mistakes of the narrator. Some suggest that the poet helplessly – or responsibly – admits himself unable to solve the problems he has raised. The question of whom Meed will marry finds only a negative and partial answer – 'Not Conscience' – and Meed fades out of the action. In the confession scene the test case of Robert the

Robber, who repents, is unable to make restitution and throws himself on the mercy of Christ, is left open: 'What bifel of þis feloun I kan noȝt faire schewe . . .' (V 471). The sinfulness of the world, the uncertainty of heaven, are ills that Langland refuses to palliate with fictional satisfactions.

Langland exploits and discards the conventions of the dream vision, jolting the complacencies the form might encourage about the safety of the waking world and the clarity of revealed knowledge. Similarly, he is prepared to thwart our narrative expectations if inconclusiveness or re-statement best serve the cause of precision. Such procedures determine the action of the second vision, where the sequence of pilgrimage, ploughing, pardon, looks less like a progression than a series of false starts. The pilgrims who 'bluster forth' to journey to 'St Truth' have, like Will in his search for Dowel, mistaken the nature of their object and pursuit. And the allegorical method might even seem to support their misapprehensions. Langland first stresses that the pilgrimage must be a symbolic one (V 561–629) but then abandons the image altogether: in a poem a metaphorical pilgrimage may look misleadingly like a literal one. Better to make the pilgrims plough and help Piers with the world's work, call the ploughman's equipment the badges of pilgrimage (VI 102–3), dramatise the suspicion of mechanical or escapist religious observance.[19] But his scrupulousness provokes disappointment as well as respect. Ideologically, it is right and satisfying that ploughing should be substituted for pilgrimage; yet, fictionally, it produces a sense of arrested purpose. The narrative structure and the structure of ideas contradict each other. Similarly, the familiar sequence of sermon, confession, pilgrimage, would have led the medieval audience to expect a pardon. During the long paraphrase in Passus VII we are encouraged to feel hopeful about the pardon. Yet when its message is revealed it is torn up. Here the mysterious authority of Piers's action shatters the didactic carefulness of the last passus. The teaching was good, clear and true but the scene dissolves in anger, violence and enigma. The vision ends with a chasm in the structure of its argument.

The poem keeps proposing but then disrupting patterns for organising experience. The Prologue and Passus I present life as a straightforward journey towards either dungeon or tower. Yet *Piers* is full of unfinished embassies and enigmatic 'departures from the action. Pilgrimages and quests are begun with great determination but abandoned or discredited. The villains defect inconsequentially: Meed and her followers, the would-be pilgrims who recognise no kin in Truth's castle, the idle who refuse to plough. But the virtues and the virtuous equally disappear when they are most needed: Piers, introduced in the *Visio* as solid and dependable, becomes more and more elusive, so that a new pilgrimage to seek him is undertaken in the last lines of the poem; Conscience refuses to stay with Clergy after the dinner; in C, Reason also bows out of the action in the same scene; Christ himself can be seen as a disappearing hero whose spirit becomes less and less operative in the militant Church.

Yet the effects of the incomplete narratives, unreliable structures, evanescent characters, are not totally negative. In this analysis I have tried to present some of the contradictions in the poem clearly; in reading they may not be so sharply felt. The problems of the pardon scene are especially difficult: Langland presumably came to think them misleadingly provocative as he omitted the tearing from the C version. Yet, insoluble as the passus appears in A and B, the drama of the tearing obscurely satisfies and the absoluteness of the dilemmas may not be immediately visible. Comparing the versions, E. T. Donaldson argues that C emends too conscientiously, irons out inconsistencies which were not destructive to the emotional logic of B. Of the tearing, he writes:

> The passage is so dramatically apt that only after thinking back does one recall, with a shock, that the pardon Piers has torn was sent him by Truth and may possibly, if Coghill's surmise is correct, represent the Atonement. Even then, most readers would prefer to keep the scene as it stands and undergo the shock of Piers's seeming ingratitude, rather than have a less vivid presentation.[20]

On the conflict between Truth's instruction to Piers at the beginning of the passus to continue the work of the half-acre and Piers's resolution at the end of it to cease from sowing, Donaldson remarks, 'I wonder how many readers have noticed the inconsistency, or, if they have, how many have let it affect their pleasure in the poem'.[21] My own experience of first reading *Piers* – and that of many students I have discussed it with – bears this out. The paradoxes of the episode are, on reflection, compounded by the further paradox of having been so readily acceptable.

One reason is that the last passus of the *Visio* is based upon another kind of double structure. The narrative both presents a clash of irreconcilable statements and unfolds as a series of affirmations. The pardon and the tearing, Truth's command and Piers's resolution, are felt, on a first reading, as positives. We are encouraged, initially, to assent to Piers's work on the half-acre and to Truth's terms in the pardon. The negations that follow are, therefore, the more violent. But we were not exactly deceived in placing trust in ploughing and pardon. We are confronted in this passus with some of the major polarities in Christian thought: law and inspiration, Church and individual, authority and mysticism. Its organisation persuades us to accept the validity of each and to experience the maximum tension between them. The strain and the passion of the climax depend upon our having given credence – and rightly – to all that preceded it. Its profundity would be lost if it were merely a simple negation. In contrast, Will's attempt on waking to play safe, believe in everything at once, deny the problems by accepting all authorities, looks flabby and superstitious.

Throughout *Piers* the abandoned narratives and enquiries disappoint. Yet their effect is inconsequential and agnostic, rather than purely desolating. If assurances of consolation are often lacking, so too are rigid schemes of judgement. Though, for example, the questions about salvation are usually unanswered, they do not receive a negative reply. The hope in a dubiously orthodox, 'barely prayable' affirmative is fulfilled: when the Dreamer asks if the unforgivable sin against the Holy Ghost could be forgiven, the Samaritan answers 'Yes' (XVII 303). Just as the locations of the action are apt to dissolve and its inhabitants to disappear, the argument is enveloped in a pervading atmosphere of vagueness which contrasts with Will's desire for categories and precision. A. C. Spearing suggests that vagueness is a positive quality in *Piers*, a reaction against the clear-cut systems and fine distinctions of late scholasticism.[22] Its intellectualism and abstraction is criticised and parodied in the presentation of the dreamer as 'a kind of amateur scholastic'. Spearing raises the issue of 'significant vagueness' in *Piers* at the end of a study of a rhetorical feature of the poem, the persistent use of verbal repetition. This is one of the subtler ways in which the poem advocates general faith in what is obviously good rather than hair-splitting theological virtuosity. This preference is also expressed in direct statements: in the criticisms of the friars, intellectuals as well as mendicants, who 'glosed þe gospel' (Prol. 60) and are advised by Conscience to give up logic and learn to love (XX 250); in Study's comment that, without love, theology would be a'lewed þyng' (X 189); in Piers's inpugning of all the sciences in favour of love alone (XIII 124–5). *Piers Plowman* is full of intellectual dilemmas, presented with great drama, argued about with angry intensity, yet it suggests that at the deepest level they do not, after all, really matter.

The formal strangeness of *Piers* also acts as a formal solution to the central problem of religious literature. Burke pointed out that a row of evenly spaced columns suggested an infinite series.[23] Similarly, the superimposition of one structure upon another, opposite in meaning, gives an impression of unfathomed depth. The ambiguity of the word 'infinite' in *Piers* is both example and description of this effect: the incomplete points to the perfect, where statement must logically fall short of it. The inconclusiveness of the poem evokes religious awe rather than scepticism. Negation can be as expressive of faith as of doubt. There is a tradition of 'negative theology' which, insisting on both the inadequacy of words to describe God and the obligation to praise him in language, simultaneously affirms, qualifies and denies.[24] As Augustine comments of the statement that the Trinity is Three Persons, we use the words '*Non ut illud diceretur, sed ne taceretur* (*De Trinitate* V 9): Not that this should be said but that it should not be left unsaid.' Mystical writers, such as Langland's contemporary, the author of *The Cloud of Unknowing*, frequently declare that they can express their apprehension of God only in terms of what he is not.

Conversely, some Christian poets – Milton, for example – have even seen in man's fallen state a basis for limited and negative understanding: conscious appreciation of goodness through knowing sin, of joy by contrast with suffering. Langland's Four Daughters of God voice this argument at the end of Passus XVIII: no weather is more beautiful than sunshine after a storm, no affection more welcome than that between reconciled friends (XVIII 409–14).

Nor is this negative and ironic use of language a literary sleight of hand by which poets evade a philosophical problem. Plato's description in the *Symposium* of Eros as loving rather than lovely, as poor, ignorant, ugly, bare-foot, is more than an attempt to disarm the 'Third Man' objection to the theory of ideal forms. The definition also rests upon deep emotional realities, on Socrates' sense of the 'strangeness' of Diotima, on Alcibiades's shame in the presence of Socrates.[25] Will's relation to Piers resembles that of Socrates to Diotima and Alcibiades to Socrates. The absences of Piers, the yearning for Piers convey, more than satisfaction could, his meaning in the poem. Human perception is inadequate: clerks – including Langland – learn through words; Piers understands the invisible and inexpressible (XV 198–200). In the poem the truth Piers represents can be manifested only in the violence of the longing for it and the rejection of all else as not it. We feel its power when, after Piers's long absence from the B *Vita*, the Dreamer faints with joy on hearing his name (XVI 18–19); Conscience bears witness to it in his departure at the end of the poem to seek for Piers.

# 3 The Christian Poet and the Christian Satirist

The conflict that I see between the atmosphere and the argument of *Piers Plowman* was probably less visible to its author. My discussion of shifting tones, of structures ironically contradicting statements, is indebted to a modern poetic which insists that what you say is, largely, how you say it. Meaning is not imported from outside and placed within the literary work; rather, it is the sum of all the aspects of the poem. 'Fruit' and 'chaff' cannot be distinguished. Paraphrase is not only inadequate but, to a greater or lesser extent, distorting. All verbal structures are unique. Some, like *Piers*, are more unique than others.

Will and Imaginatif, however, discuss *Piers* in terms of subject, paraphraseable content and what it has in common with other literary works (XII 16–29). Their conversation implies that the form the poem was taking perplexed its author but Imaginatif's criticisms seem to bypass its most problematic features. He claims that its message is readily available elsewhere, that there are already books and teachers to tell men of Dowel, Dobet and Dobest. If the poem edifies through its Christian teaching, he cannot see what peculiar value is to be placed upon it. From Imaginatif's objection one might infer that *Piers Plowman* was a conventional re-statement of Christian truisms. And, if *Piers* is thus to be reduced to its doctrinal content, its power to distress and disturb both reader and author remains inexplicable.

How could the transmission of orthodox Christian teaching do other than console? I have suggested, by some internal analysis of the poem's strategies, that *Piers* subverts the consolations it affirms, that it simultaneously means opposites. Langland expresses his uneasiness about the poem in external terms: that its purpose is served by other books, that his life might be better spent than in composing it, that he is not a worthy author of a sacred poem.

I find this conversation between Will and Imaginatif the most tantalising in *Piers Plowman*. It is quite free from Langland's more usual faults: it is not obscure, rambling or digressive. Imaginatif states concisely that Will is wasting time composing the poem when he should be praying for his benefactors and when there are already many sources from which people can learn of Dowel, Dobet and Dobest. Will replies clearly that the authority of Cato and the examples of the lives of saints sanction play as well as work and that, if he could find out about Dowel, Dobet and Dobest, he would devote himself to prayer. By the general conversational standards of *Piers* this is a lucid exchange. Yet I think it more seriously thwarting than, for example, the much re-written speech of Wit on the three states of goodness or than Anima's meandering discourse on Charity. Here we might learn what Langland thought of the function and value of poetry and we are disappointed. Will's reply is at best a *non sequitur*, a comment on his spiritual condition rather than his role as poet. At worst, it capitulates to the most narrowly didactic view of literature.

It is obviously perverse to wish that Langland had offered an apology for poetry in terms which would completely satisfy a modern literary theorist. No medieval poet did or could have done. Yet the only cogent refutation of Imaginatif's view that praying is always a better activity than writing and that other books serve exactly the same function as *Piers* would be a defence of the poem as *poem*. That Imaginatif makes such accusations while Langland continued to write the poem suggests a psychological conflict: Langland felt the need of such a justification even if he could not precisely formulate it. And the strategies of the poem provide abundant evidence for the view that each use of language is unique: Langland shows in his treatment of such words as 'meed', 'wit', 'wisdom', 'cardinal' that context determines meaning; he demonstrates through his exhausted but indefatigable Dreamer that 'truth' must be felt as experience rather than learned as lesson; he compels the reader to endure, with Will, mistakes, confusion and indirection in the search for understanding. His methods are not those of a man who regards poem as statement. Despite the suggestions that the poem is autobiographical, Langland uses, as much as later writers of 'anti-novels', techniques which draw attention to the fictionality of the poem: an ambiguity between the author as controlling creator and helpless, criticised character within his own work. *Piers* is a deeply earnest poem and there is in it no element of literary joke. Nevertheless, Langland's solutions of the problem of being a sinful ignorant creature as well as an omniscient author have analogies in comic and overtly aesthetic ironies. Although these are more common in modern fiction, there is an obvious medieval parallel in *The Canterbury Tales*: Chaucer, creator of all the characters and their stories, is silenced and ridiculed by some of the other pilgrims as the least competent story-teller in the cast.

Of Langland's contemporaries Chaucer is the most obviously conscious and sophisticated in his attitude to language and to his stance as poet. In *The World and the Book*,[1] a study of pre- and post-Renaissance philosophies of literature, Gabriel Josipovici takes Chaucer as his first 'modern' author and discusses the relativism of his presentation of character, his scepticism of the authority of the written word and his awareness of the fictive quality of all human utterance. In contrast, Josipovici describes Langland as the medieval norm: an author secure in his faith in the world outside him and in the objectivity of words in books. I find this picture of Langland unrecognisable. And, while *The World and the Book* is usually as perceptive as it is learned, and its account of Chaucer's implied dubieties about books is unsurpassed, I think that its portrait of a subjectivist Chaucer should also be qualified. Chaucer is more faithful, Langland less trusting than Josipovici allows.

*Troilus and Criseyde* handles, with supreme tact and brilliance, the major problems of authorship and epistemology. It used often to be described, in a crude commonplace, as 'the first modern novel' for its moments of naturalism and its effect of psychological authenticity. I find that it resembles much modern fiction not in seeming 'real' but in questioning what 'reality' is. It should be impossible to read *Troilus* without being aware that the story is being narrated and perhaps refracted and that the different styles employed by the three major characters imply their different views of love and truth.[2] Are love and truth absolutes? And, if they are, could we know it? The prologue to Book II of *Troilus*, shelving responsibility on to the (wrong) 'auctour', points to the relativity of human speech and behaviour:

Ye knowe ek that in forme of speche is chaunge
Withinne a thousand yeer, and wordes tho
That hadden pris, now wonder nyce and straunge
Us thinketh hem, and yet thei spake hem so,
And spedde as wel in love as men now do;
Ek for to wynnen love in sondry ages,
In sondry londes, sondry ben usages . . .

Ek scarsly ben ther in this place thre
That have in love seid lik, and don, in al;
For to thi purpos this may liken the,
And the right nought, yet al is seid or schal;
Ek some men grave in tree, some in ston wal,
As it bitit; but syn I have bigonne,
Myn auctour shal I folwen, if I konne.

*Troilus*, II 22–8, 43–9

Conventions vary, in different periods and in different countries; human language itself changes, so that words become obsolete or alter in meaning; even among Chaucer's contemporary English audience there are such divergencies of personality that its members will express love in various ways: to use a metaphor from visual art, some sculptors carve in wood, some in stone. But a central question remains unanswered: is love the same experience for all these people? Or do the differences in expression reflect differences of feeling? Can the artist say the same things in wood as in stone? The author's silence on these matters gives an effect of agnosticism unusual in his period.

But, powerful though this effect is in *Troilus*, we should not think it Chaucer's exclusive position. In the sublunary world of human love he points out that our hold on reality is slippery, that our perceptions are no sure guide to truth. Yet, in the prologue to Book II, he uses a religious as well as an aesthetic metaphor: 'For every wight, which that to Rome went/Halt not o path, or alwey o manere' (*Troilus*, II 36–7). There are many ways of pilgrimage to Rome but presumably the destination and its meaning are constant. The epilogue to *Troilus* with its affirmation of trust in immutable love and truth and dismissal of the changing, fading beauty of human affections is, perhaps, too critically problemátic itself to serve as witness to Chaucer's faith in an absolute. But a passage from *The Canterbury Tales* contrasts suggestively with the view of language proposed in Book II of *Troilus*:

It is a moral tale vertuous,
Al be it told somtyme in sondry wyse
Of sondry folk, as I shal yow devyse.
   As thus: ye woot that every Evaungelist,
That telleth us the peyne of Jhesu Crist,
He seith nat alle thyng as his felawe dooth;
But nathelees hir sentence is al sooth,
And alle acorden as in hire sentence,
Al be ther in hir tellyng difference.
For some of hem seyn moore, and somme seyn lesse,
Whan they his pitous passioun expresse –
I meene of Mark, Mathew, Luc, and John –
But doutelees hir sentence is al oon.

                                        *CT* VII 940–52

Here, as in *Troilus*, we are reminded that 'sondry' people speak in 'sondry' ways but here we are instructed not to pay too much attention to the fact. The Evangelists give different accounts of the Passion but their 'sentence' is the same. In matters central to faith, meaning is more powerful than the words which express it and can even communicate itself with some independence from them. Chaucer can allow vagaries of interpretation in secular but not in sacred literature.

Langland, writing a sacred poem, regards the ambiguities

of language not as creatively fruitful but as symptomatic of a fallen world. He first expresses the opposition between good and evil, God and Satan, as a conflict between Truth and Falsehood. The false exploits the ambiguous, a problem dramatised most fully in the attempt to define Meed. Here misunderstanding and misuse of language imperil both the individual soul and the stability of the kingdom. The confessions of the Deadly Sins can be vitiated by their failure to grasp the moral vocabulary of repentance: Avarice 'wende riflynge were restitucion' (V 235); Envy is 'sory . . . for I ne may me venge' (V 128–9). One of Will's handicaps in the *Vita* is his grammatical misconstruction of the phrase 'do well'. In the Harrowing of Hell, Christ accuses Satan of achieving man's fall by 'deceite . . . with gile . . . falsliche' (XVIII 333, 334, 336). Pride's assault on the Church in *Dobest* is conducted largely through perversions of language and attack on meaning: the sense of the cardinal virtues is distorted (XIX 455–64); Anti-Christ turns upside down the crop of Truth and 'made fals sprynge and sprede' (XX 54–5). Satanic guile infects all human use of language. Throughout the poem Langland has pilloried the deceitful speech of various people: friars, pilgrims, merchants, lawyers, beggars. Are poets also guilty of corruption of language?[3]

Langland never expresses his view of poetry fully and directly, though, during the composition of his poem, it seems to become increasingly suspicious and austere. In C the part of the conversation with Imaginatif which treats of the poem is omitted. The argument about the value of Will's work takes place in the 'autobiographical' episode, in which Reason and Conscience accuse the narrator of idleness and of criticising 'lolleres' for faults which he himself shares. If this interrogation replaces the discussion of poetry with Imaginatif, the problem of the value of literature receives even less attention. Here the emphasis is not on whether writing poetry is a waste of time compared with praying but on whether any valid occupation can be discerned in the unstructured nature of Will's life.

Langland's attitude towards his role as poet has, for the most part, to be extrapolated from his general views on the use and misuse of language and from his particular preoccupation with the subject of minstrels. The re-written

speech of Imaginatif in C opens with almost the same line as
B: 'Ich haue yfolwed þe in faiþ more þan fourty wynter' (C
XV 3) but he continues quite differently:

> And wissede þe ful ofte what dowel was to mene,
> And counsailede þe for cristes sake no creature to by-gyle,
> Noþer to lye noþer to lacke ne lere þat is defendid
> Ne to spille speche as to speke an ydel,
> And no tyme to tyne ne trewe þyng to teenen;
> Lowe þe to lyve forth in þe lawe of holychurche;
> Þenne dost þow wel, with-oute drede, ho can do bet,
> no forse!
>
> C XV 5–10

Here Imaginatif, a function of Will's intellect, states firmly
that he knows the meaning of Dowel and thus implicitly
disarms the narrator of the second defence of the poem
which he used in B. And, although the specific attack on
poetry has been dropped, Langland's doubts about his
writing may be inferred from the negative advice given here
to those who would do well: not to criticise, not to speak
falsely or attack anything true, not to teach what is forbidden, not to waste speech or time, not to utter idle words. The
dangers of learning, that it may lead to excessive curiosity,
irresponsible dispute and heretical speculation, are evidently
seen as occupational hazards for the poet. In the rest of this
chapter I shall discuss the implications for *Piers* of the
prohibitions on 'spilling speech' and on criticising. Langland
seems to have feared that the composition of the poem was
involving him in both these forbidden activities.

The idea of waste of speech evidently worried Langland
and he mentions it increasingly during the second and third
versions of the poem. It is specifically condemned in the New
Testament when Jesus predicts that we shall have to answer
on the Day of Judgement for every idle word we ever spoke
(*Matthew*, XII, 36), a monition which, taken earnestly, would
prevent most human communication. For the poet it entails
a responsibility greater than the need to avoid pointless
chatter: it reminds him also of the grim warning of the
parable of the talents. If all speech is of divine origin and
should not be abused, a particular obligation must be felt by

those whom God has made unusually articulate, those to
whom 'he yaf wit with wordes to shewe,/To wynne wiþ
truþe . . . by wit to wissen oþere as grace hem wolde teche.'
(XIX 229–33). Wit, the faculty repeatedly stressed in this
account of God's distribution of talent, condemns waste of
speech and links it, in a resonant metaphor, with cacoph-
onous music and debauched minstrelsy:

> Tynynge of tyme, truþe woot þe soþe,
> Is moost yhated vpon erþe of hem þat ben in heuene;
> And siþþe to spille speche þat spire is of grace
> And goddes gleman and a game of heuene.
> Wolde neuere þe feiþful fader his fiþele were vntempred
> Ne his gleman a gedelyng, a goere to tauernes.
>
> IX 101–6

Imaginatif in B, Reason and Conscience in C, accuse Will
of wasting time while he writes his poem. May he also be
'spilling speech'? Even if poems are not subversive, obscene
or heretical, are they (despite Cato's advice to his son)
permissible as entertainment? Langland's pre-occupation
with the moral status of minstrelsy, his continual attempts to
distinguish between good and bad minstrels, suggest a fear
that he may be misusing his talent. From Langland's apparently chaotic treatment of this subject E. T. Donaldson has
produced a brilliantly ordered account of his problems and
the evolution of his thought about minstrels. Donaldson
finds that the author's perplexity produces contradictions
both within each version of the poem and between all three,
that his attitude towards minstrelsy becomes increasingly
austere but that in C he is encouraged by the Franciscan
tradition of inspired poets as *joculatores Domini* to place some
faith in the possibility of sacred poetry.[4]

Donaldson's discussion of this subject is comprehensive
and convincing and I could not improve upon it. I shall
quote one passage, at the end of XIII, which raises the major
problems about minstrelsy voiced elsewhere and often in all
three texts of *Piers*:

> Ye lordes and ladies and legates of holy chirche
> That fedeþ fooles sages, flatereris and lieris,

And han likynge to liþen hem in hope to do yow lauȝe –
*Ve vobis qui ridetis &c.* –
And ȝyueþ hem mete and mede, and pouere men refuse,
In youre deeþ deyinge I drede me soore
Lest þo þre maner men to muche sorwe yow brynge:
*Consencientes & agentes pari pena punientur.*
Patriarkes and prophetes, prechours of goddes wordes,
Sauen þoruȝ hir sermon mannes soule fro helle;
Riȝt so flatereris and fooles arn þe fendes disciples
To entice men þoruȝ hir tales to synne and harlotrie.

                                                    XIII 421–30

This passage obviously condemns the abuse of speech: mock
wisdom, flattery, falsehood, utterance of amusing frivolities
rather than the word of God. Its moral dangers are far-
reaching: those who connive at a sin are as guilty as those
who first commit it. Unworthy minstrels, by diverting charity from the poor, share the blame for the economic injustice
of society; they are, by implication, analogous to the beggars
who receive alms on false pretences. The guilt of entertainers
and audience is reciprocal: the minstrels provoke evil
responses and reactions; their patrons encourage the sinfulness of the minstrels by listening to them. Misuse of minstrelsy is not a trivial diversion: it is the *opposite* of holy
teaching. Prophets and preachers use language to save men
from hell; flatterers and fools are the disciples of the devil
and lead men to hell. Even laughter is condemned: there was
a medieval tradition, alluded to in C (C III 32), that in his life
on earth Christ never laughed.

The passage continues with a metaphorical definition of
worthy minstrels which would seem to rule out virtually all
literal minstrels as unworthy:

Clerkes and kniȝtes welcomeþ kynges minstrales,
And for loue of hir lorde liþeþ hem at festes;
Muche moore, me þynkeþ, riche men scholde
Haue beggeres bifore hem þe whiche ben goddes min-
    strales
As he seiþ hymself; seynt Iohan bereþ witnesse;
    *Qui vos spernit, me spernit.*
Forþi I rede yow riche, reueles whan ye makeþ,

For to solace youre soules swiche minstrales to haue:
The pouere for a fool sage syttyng at þi table,
And a lered man, to lere þee what our lord suffred,
For to saue þi soule from sathan þyn enemy,
And fiþele þee wiþoute flateryng of good friday þe geste,
And a blynd man for a bourdeour, or a bedrede womman
To crie a largesse bifore oure lord, youre good loos
    to shewe.
Thise þre maner minstrales makeþ a man to lauȝe,
And, in his deeþ deyinge þei don hym gret confort
That by his lyue liþed hem and loued hem to here.

XIII 436–51

Here, as in Hawkin's description of himself as an honest
minstrel incapable of performing the entire repertoire of his
profession (XIII 228–34), the metaphor insists on opposition
rather than analogy. 'God's minstrels' here are not even the
*joculatores Domini* of Franciscan tradition: they are inarticu-
late beggars. 'Solace' is to be found not in amusement or
beauty but in the contemplation of suffering. Heavenly
values reverse worldly social categories: spiritually, the poor
should sit at the high table and the blind man and the
bed-ridden woman will intercede with the Lord and ask
alms for the rich. The blind man fills the role of jester.
Meditation on pain will make one 'laugh' in some pure sense
which bears little or no relation to earthly laughter. A violent
assault is being made on our normal emotions and the
language in which we express them: Hamlet's sardonic
remark to Yorick's skull, 'Make her laugh at that', assumes
the infinity of a gulf which Langland urges us to bridge.

In this definition of 'true' minstrelsy the learned man's
account of the Passion is the only verbal element permitted.
Sacred literature is approved, though not thought pre-
eminent, as a form of spiritual education. On these terms
*Piers Plowman* itself might be acceptable: it is a religious and
didactic work, unflattering to the rich (and to most other
people), and it recounts the life of Christ and the story of
Good Friday. Yet the two lines on the learned man's Biblical
teaching do not sound at all self-descriptive. They occur in
the context of a poem which has questioned the value of
learning as a spiritual force, even though it criticises itself for

voicing this criticism. This is one example of the contrast between *Piers* and the hypothetical religious work which it here applauds. The learned man's prose or verse narrative of the Passion sounds very 'straight': like the instruction of Holy Church in Passus I, it tells Christians what they already know. Its simplicity would rebuke, by implication, the involutions and indirectness of *Piers Plowman*. The learned man would sing without flattering his audience and, presumably, without flattering himself: his re-telling of a sacred narrative would be humbly and devoutly second-hand. By contrast, the originality of *Piers*, the intrusiveness of its author's personality and problems, might well seem dangerously 'busy' and self-interested.

*Piers Plowman* also raises the question of whether satire is more, or less, morally dubious than other kinds of poetry. Imaginatif says, in C, that it is no part of Dowel to criticise others and malicious gossip bulks large in the self-incrimination of Hawkin in C and the confessions of the Seven Deadly Sins in B.[5] Hawkin is guilty of 'scornyng and of scoffyng' (XIII 276), 'lakkyng lettrede men and lewed men boþe' (XIII 286), he tells 'al þat he wiste wikked by any wight' (XIII 323) and loves to 'blame men bihynde hir bak' (XIII 324). Anger delights in scandal: he makes 'Ioutes of Ianglyng' (V 158); he confesses 'Al þe wikkednesse þat I woot by any of oure breþeren,/I couȝe it vp in oure Cloistre þat al þe Couent woot it' (V 180–1). Envy traduces his neighbour, turns friends into enemies and continually foments murderous quarrels with his talk (V 93–100). The evils and dangers of such behaviour are obvious.

Yet the Christian is also obliged to speak out against abuses, not to be guilty of 'unsittynge suffraunce' (C IV 208). He must hate the sin while loving the sinner, attack vice as well as promote virtue. The tension this may cause is a version, on the human scale, of the larger paradox of God's simultaneous perfection of justice and mercy. Here, too, both elements of the paradox have Biblical support. In the Old Testament God says 'Vengeance is mine; I will repay'; in the New Testament Christ enjoins 'Judge not, that ye be not judged'. Yet both Testaments show examples of righteous indignation: Moses' anger at the idolatry of the Israelites;[6] Christ's forcible expulsion of the money-changers from the temple.

In *Complaint and Satire in Early English Literature*[7] John Peter argues that this was a dilemma for early Christian writers which had been resolved by the later medieval period. St Jerome, for example, could not reconcile the ideal of Christian mildness with the Roman tradition of violent satire. Jerome 'has little to say for . . . mildness, and he even brushes aside the commandment "Judge not", with a brief comment explaining that it is not a prohibition but an injunction to judge justly.' But in the eleventh century the equally irascible St. Peter Damian felt no need for such excuses: 'The antithesis that had so perplexed Jerome – *"Irasci hominis est, injuriam non facere Christiani"* – has lost its force by the time we come to Damian. A whole literature has grown up to validate the concept of an indignation that is specifically Christian, and thus perfectly defensible, and to govern its expression'.[8] This literature is, in Peter's terminology, not Satire, but Complaint. Whereas Satire is vivid, personal, particular and may even betray a vicious delight in corruption on the part of the satirist, Complaint is generalised, repetitive, hortatory and expresses melancholy regret for the state of fallen man.

A passage from Langland's confession of Sloth is Peter's first example of Complaint and foundation for his definition of the term.[9] But I cannot agree with his implicit denial that Langland felt any unease about his denunciations of others and, indeed, throughout his discussion of later medieval literature Peter keeps treating *Piers Plowman* as an exception.[10] The conversation with Lewte in Passus XI expresses Will's doubts about the morality of public criticism of others and shows that Langland knew, as well as earlier Christian writers, the apparent contradictions of the Bible on this subject:

> And lewte lou3 on me for I loured on þe frere;
> 'Wherfore lourestow?' quod lewtee, and loked on me harde.
> 'If I dorste', quod I, 'amonges men þis metels auowe!'
> '3is, by Peter and by Poul!' quod he and took hem boþe to witnesse:
> *Non oderis fratres secrete in corde tuo set publice argue illos.*

'They wole aleggen also', quod I, 'and by þe gospel
preuen:
*Nolite iudicare quemquam.'*

XI 84–90

The Dreamer is afraid to reveal the corruption of the friars.
Lewte cites, punningly, a text from Scripture to prove that
one should not hate the sinner but should publicly expose
the sin. Will replies that the friars are equally apt at quoting
Scripture and, in this case, have unambiguous authority for
silencing critics. Lewte, however, maintains that open cen-
sure is, with some provisos, desirable:

'And wherof serueþ lawe', quod lewtee, 'if no lif vnder-
toke it
Falsnesse ne faiterie? for somwhat þe Apostle seide
*Non oderis fratrem.*
And in þe Sauter also seiþ dauid þe prophete
*Existimasti inique quod ero tui similis &c.*
It is *licitum* for lewed men to legge þe soþe
If hem likeþ and lest; ech a lawe it graunteþ,
Excepte persons and preestes and prelates of holy chirche.
It falleþ noȝt for þat folk no tales to telle
Thouȝ þe tale were trewe, and it touched synne.
Þyng þat al þe world woot, wherfore sholdestow spare
To reden it in Retorik to arate dedly synne?
Ac be þow neueremoore þe firste þe defaute to blame;
Thouȝ þow se yuel seye it noȝt first; be sory it nere
amended.
Thyng þat is pryue, publice þow it neuere,
Neiþer for loue looue it noȝt ne lakke it for enuye;
*Parum lauda; vitupera parcius'*

XI 91–106

The moral law would be inoperative if no one would
condemn wrong-doing. But there are some circumstances in
which denunciation is improper: by the clergy (presumably
because of the secrecy of the confessional); when it would
reveal something previously unknown; if the critic takes any
pleasure in the corruption he attacks or if his praise and
blame are influenced by his own likes and dislikes. Lewte

repeats the New Testament text which advises open engagement with *'fratres'* and backs it up with a rather self-righteous quotation from the Psalter. Scripture immediately approves Lewte's speech and confirms that he is telling the truth (XI 107).

What Lewte recommends, the castigation of known evils arousing no pleasure in their critic, accords exactly with Peter's definition of Complaint. Lewte's prescription would also produce the monotonous effect of Complaint, of the same laments over the same abuses repeated through the centuries. One may wonder if the most useful criticism is of what is already generally known. Peter's account of the stability of Complaint, of its perpetual grieving over the fallen state of man, emphasises the elegiac rather than the corrective tone. Yet the satire in *Piers Plowman* is frequently irascible in tone and chooses specific and contemporary objects: Will has to be reminded that men are frail and that, in a fallen world, their sinfulness is natural and must be treated gently (XI 379–94). It is difficult to accept that Langland felt his criticism of others to be obviously morally correct: the discussion with Lewte occurs at the 'join', in the passus where B re-writes the end of A. It may express one of the problems, like the questions about learning and salvation, which had prevented Langland from finishing A and caused the long delay before he undertook B.

There is another moral issue for the Christian satirist which Peter does not discuss but which obviously concerned Langland. The Bible warns against seeing the mote in your brother's eye, while ignoring the beam in your own. Inevitably, the superior stance adopted by the satirist, amateur or professional, encourages presumption. Hawkin criticises others 'Willynge þat men wende his wit were þe best . . . And noon so holy as he ne of lif clennere' (XIII 291, 295). Reason advises the Dreamer: 'rule þi tonge bettre,/And er þow lakke my lif loke þyn be to preise!' (XI 387–8). In C Reason and Conscience ask if the critic of 'lolleres' may not be equally idle and unproductive. The *Visio* continually advocates hard work, the *Vita* celebrates patience, but Will is possibly indolent and certainly contentious. Langland's solution – a painful one if his narrator is in part a self-portrait – is in the irony of his presentation of Will, in the reflexive quality of his attacks on imperfect clerks, bad minstrels, proud critics, words without works, abuse of the divine gift of language.

*Piers* is not primarily a satirical work. Yet it is only on the question of satire that Langland can formulate the problem latent in the entire poem: that one might say the right thing in the wrong way or with the wrong motives; that the 'personality' of a literary work may colour its doctrine'. It is the clearest – if crudest – example of the paradoxical use of language, the duality or plurality of effect, which is so characteristic and mysterious in *Piers Plowman*.

# 4 Abstract and Concrete

In the last chapters of this study I shall discuss some objections which may be made to allegory and which I think Langland confronted in his writing and re-writing of *Piers*. The relationship between abstract and concrete vocabulary is obviously central to the allegorical mode. An examination of Langland's handling of abstract and concrete suggests that the tension between them is very fully exploited in *Piers*. In this chapter I shall consider some passages which present sharp lexical contrasts of this kind. I shall argue that Langland felt both respect and contempt for the material world of sense data, that he was sometimes critical of abstract thought as potentially facile but always viewed it as spiritually essential. From his treatment of abstract and concrete vocabulary one can begin to construct a theory of allegory; for Langland these lexical relationships and the allegorical mode express a Christian theology of body and soul, of fallen world and divine Incarnation.

People who like allegory praise the vividness and solidity with which it 'realises' emotional states or philosophical concepts. In *The Allegory of Love* C. S. Lewis argues that the allegorical mode was the perfect vehicle for the expression of Christian awareness of psychological conflict. He comments, discussing *Le Roman de la Rose*, that all lovers have met 'Danger' and that the garden the narrator enters conveys piercingly the feeling of being in love.[1] This particular strength of the mode could be exhaustively illustrated from *Piers Plowman*. To choose one obvious example, the confes-

sions of the Seven Deadly Sins have been much antholo-
gised and celebrated for being very 'concrete': the burgeoning
of detail in, for instance, the description of Envy – his friar's
sleeves, his resemblance to a leek withered in the sun, his
ruined appetite (V 80, 81, 121–24) – embodies the misery,
the ugliness, the perils of being envious.

People who dislike allegory condemn it as static, tautological and full of 'frigid abstractions'. Dr. Johnson dismissed
it thus: 'Fame tells a tale and Victory hovers over a general or
perches on a standard; but Fame and Victory can do no
more.'[2] Johnson was reacting against the frequently inert
personifications of eighteenth-century poetry; one may
observe, in passing, that Fama in the *Aeneid* and Rumour as
Prologue to *Henry IV*, Part II, do a great deal more. Angus
Fletcher analyses this kind of doubt about allegory with
more subtlety:

> Allegory is usually said to be "abstract" because it uses
> "personified abstractions". But allegory is much more
> profoundly abstract than in the mere use of animate
> philosophical terms. It is abstract in Whitehead's sense,
> when he says that abstraction is "the omission of part of
> the truth." It is abstract in the sense of suppressing part of
> the conditions relevant to its subjects and objects. An
> allegory of Justice, for example, will omit the contingen-
> cies that make a non-repressive, tolerant justice so difficult
> to achieve. It omits the human detail, which the mimetic
> mode, and its highly condensed form, the mythical mode,
> do not omit. "Abstraction" in allegory also has the mean-
> ing of "abstracted behaviour" – behaviour that lacks the
> full breadth and excitement of human involvement.
> Allegory often has "an abstracted air".[3]

I shall argue in later chapters that Langland shows himself
very aware of the ease with which the allegorical mode can
beg questions and, questioning, sometimes sabotages his
own allegory. But one could illustrate what Fletcher
describes from *Piers*. When the Dreamer asks Holy Church
about the ownership of money, she quotes the text *Reddite
Caesari* and states:

. . . For riȝtfully reson sholde rule yow alle,
And kynde wit be wardeyn youre welþe to kepe
And tutour of your tresor, and take it yow at nede;
For housbondrie and he holden togidres.　　　　I 54–7

Her abstractions, 'reason', 'kind wit' and 'husbandry', sound authoritative but are not particularly helpful. Will has asked how to use money rightly; Holy Church replies, in effect, 'Use money rightly'. The generality of her advice omits the 'contingencies' and 'human detail' which make economic justice difficult to define and achieve in individual cases.

At this point Holy Church might retort to me, as Imaginatif later does to Will, that there are already plenty of other books which explain what doing well is. She need only allude to the names of good qualities which are fully defined elsewhere. Turning from ethics to poetry, I should admit that my distaste for this passage may be unsympathetically modern, not in a lack of trust in general precepts, but in a dislike of abstract words doing all the work. Medieval poetry is much more hospitable than modern to abstractions. In the twentieth century many poems and poetics – Imagist theory, the influence of Eliot's phrase 'objective correlative', the rather self-conscious refusal of the Movement poets to make large claims for their art, the subjectivity of confessional poets, 'concrete' poetry itself – have encouraged us to feel that the proper texture of poetry is local and individual. I cannot think of any abstract words which are central for modern poets, which by their own importance carry the same weight and receive as much meditative scrutiny as, for example, 'truth' and 'courtesy' in fourteenth-century poetry.

By way of corrective and before discussing Langland's more complex treatment of abstract and concrete vocabulary, I should like to indicate how a short anonymous fourteenth-century religious lyric proceeds largely and very movingly through a series of abstractions:

Wyth what mastrie
He hat man ywroht,
Wyth what curtaysie
He ys to man ybroht,

Wyth what marchandie
He hat ybouht
And what seynorie
He hat to man ythouht.[4]


Here we are invited to consider the magnitude of four abstract words, 'mastrie', 'curtaysie', 'marchandie', 'seynorie', to whose importance we are supposed already to have assented. The poem is organised in four two-line clauses, in each of which the vital abstraction ends the first line. The introductory phrases, 'wyth what', 'and what', assume that the audience has already given reverent thought to these terms and shares a sense of their meaning with the poet. But the structure, syntax and vocabulary of the poem reveal anew the power and the complexity of these abstract words. They are made dynamic in the relationships of nouns to appropriate verbs, 'hat . . . ywrouht', 'ys . . . ybroht', 'hat ybouht', 'hat ythouht', also placed in a dominant position in the rhyming second line of each clause. Three of these verbs are active, one is significantly passive: the 'courtesy' of the Incarnation is expressed grammatically in the Lord's willingness to be patient rather than agent, to suffer. All four nouns have worldly as well as spiritual connotations, suggesting that the divine can be partially apprehended through human experience, that God and man can co-operate. This is particularly striking in the case of 'marchandie', a word suspect and corruptible in human society, which nevertheless serves as metaphor, in English and Latin, for redemption. The series of abstract words begins and ends with two rather similar in meaning, 'mastrie' and 'seynorie', but their application is quite different: in the first clause God employs his mastery in creating man, in the last he entrusts lordship to him. The abstractions, presented so briefly and delicately, evoke the major doctrines of Christian theology and invite fresh realisation of them.

Like the author of this lyric, Langland presents abstract words, hallowed by Christian tradition, for our contemplation. Piers, for example, tells the pilgrims the names of seven sisters, the porters of the castle of Truth, mentioning their role and importance with the utmost brevity:

> That oon hatte Abstinence, and humilite anoþer;
> Charite and Chastite ben hire chief maydenes;
> Pacience and pees muche peple þei helpeþ;
> Largenesse þe lady let in wel manye . . .
>
> V 620–3

The economy of this passage implies that we should already know what these qualities are and why Piers recommends them so seriously. But the narrative immediately denies that such understanding can be taken for granted. Piers says that those related to the seven will be welcomed at the castle; a cutpurse and an apeward reply instantly that they have no kin there (V 630–1). The allegory maintains, of course, that people engaged in such occupations do not practise these virtues; the form of the conversation also suggests that they do not even understand what the words mean.

The cutpurse and the apeward have many kin among the folk on the field. At the beginning of the first vision Will sees the tower of Truth, the dungeon of Hell and, between them, the arena of human life in a scheme as clear-cut as that of a morality play. The introduction to the dream in C stresses the generality of Will's survey by adding a list of the abstractions he beholds:

> Al þe welþe of þis worlde & þe woo boþe
> Wynkyng as it were wyterly ich saw hyt,
> Of tryuþe & of tricherye of tresoun and of gyle . . .
>
> C I 10–12

But the comprehensive viewpoint initially granted to the narrator is not shared by many of the inhabitants of the Prologue. Most of them seem unaware of their precarious position between tower and dungeon, blind to moral absolutes and caring only for worldly values. Holy Church points this out to Will in her opening speech:

> . . . sone, slepestow? sestow þis peple,
> How bisie þei ben aboute þe maȝe?
> The mooste partie of þis peple þat passeþ on þis erþe,

Haue þei worship in þis world þei kepe no bettre;
Of ooþer heuene þan here holde þei no tale.

                                                      I 5–9

People are transients, they 'pass' through their life on earth,
the tower and dungeon are visible to Church and narrator,
yet most men behave as though this world were all.

The opening lines of the vision present a brief map of life
on earth and life after death. And they share some of the
abstract qualities of a map: they present, as if from an aerial
viewpoint, a true but simple picture of the terrain, useful in
providing directions precisely because the experience of the
travellers is more detailed and confusing. Much of the
Prologue lists, categorises and delivers decisive moral judg-
ments. Yet its phantasmagoric presentation of literal and
allegorical characters dramatises their confusion. So too does
the apparent vagueness of its choices between abstract and
concrete vocabulary, beginning with the major opposition of
those who put themselves to plough[5] and those who put
themselves to pride. During the course of the Prologue the
firm spatial relationships established at the opening dissolve
and with them the simple clarity of vision they symbolised.
By the end of the Prologue we no longer feel that the
dreamer is observing from outside and above; rather, that he
is part of the life of a busy street, jostled by the crowd and
deafened by the cries of the vendors, involved himself in 'þe
mase'. Holy Church comes *down* (I 4) from the tower to
explain to him what he has seen and rebukes him for his lack
of understanding.

In Passus XI Will is granted another panoramic view of
life, the vision of Middle Earth. Although its content is even
broader, the whole of nature rather than merely human
society, it follows a similar pattern. The narrator is first given
a superior vantage point but is finally exposed as a creature
who does not understand the meaning of what he has seen,
who exemplifies the confusion he condemns. This effect is
achieved partly through the treatment of abstract vocabulary
at the beginning and end of the vision. Will is shown the
whole of creation from the commanding position of a mountain. As well as sun and sea, birds and animals, he observes
humanity:

Man and his make I my3te se boþe,
Pouerte and plentee, boþe pees and werre,
Blisse and bale boþe I sei3 at ones,
And how men token Mede and Mercy refused.

XI 331–4

Here, as in the introduction of the terms 'wealth' and 'woe', 'truth' and 'treachery', 'treason' and 'guile' into the C Prologue, the abstract vocabulary suggests that the narrator has a comprehensive view and a clear conceptual framework in which to judge what he sees. 'Man and his make' are types, representative of all men and women; the Dreamer gazes at all their experience of wealth and deprivation, peace and war, happiness and suffering. At first sight the fourth line seems to present an equally clear opposition, of 'Mede' and 'Mercy', and a condemnation of people's preference for Meed as an obviously wrong choice. But the subject is now 'men' rather than 'man', individual cases. And we already know, from the debate in the first vision of the poem, that Meed is a very tricky concept. I shall discuss this debate in some detail in the next chapter. Here I would point out that 'Meed' can be apprehended as an abstract or a concrete word, as a concept or as a sum of money. The line may suggest that men choose material rather than spiritual gain, or that they claim to have earned reward rather than implore mercy, or (an interpretation supported by the events of the first vision) that they are lost in the ambiguities of the word 'Meed'. Specific moral choices often depend upon an understanding of abstract terms which is very difficult to achieve. The Dreamer's painful discovery in this Vision – 'þat moost meued me and my mood chaunged,' (XI 369) – is that men often lack reason. But he himself, as we learn from a nice play on words, is no exception. 'I haue wonder in my wit, þat witty art holden,/Why þow ne sewest man and his make . . .' (XI 374–5). A mere human challenges a great abstraction and stumbles into the most unreasonable remark he could make about it: he suggests, priding himself on his own 'wit', that Reason's reputation for being 'witty' is undeserved. At the beginning of the vision of Middle Earth the Dreamer handled abstract words with confidence; at the end he angrily implies that this abstraction is a contradiction in terms.

Throughout *Piers* abstractions are respected but their complexity of reference and human difficulty in understanding them are also stressed. The narrator's problems with abstract thought are shared by many of the other characters, perhaps by all human beings. Holy Church may see the choice between serving God and Mammon as a clear antithesis:

> And what man takeþ Mede, myn heed dar I legge,
> That he shal lese for hire loue a lippe of *Caritatis*.
>
> II 34–5

Literally, one cannot opt for both charity and dishonest profit. But the two words 'Mede' and '*caritatis*' have far more resonance than my paraphrase. The allegorical marriage of Meed is anticipated in the word 'loue', in the specialised sense of 'taketh' as 'takes to wed' and in the sexual connotations of 'lippe'.[6] The appeal of the visible is also contrasted with the importance of the invisible: *caritas* is scarcely personified and 'Mede' suggests a pile of gold coins as well as the plausible captive of the first vision. 'Mede' here seems concrete and palpable, '*caritas*' abstract and mysterious, its numinous quality emphasised by the Latin form of the word. Yet Meed, as we are to learn, is also mysterious: Holy Church's direct opposition of Meed to Charity does not allow for the ambiguities which will deceive not only the King but even Theology itself.

Although Langland fully sees the problems inherent in abstract vocabulary, he frequently uses concrete words with distaste to evoke the perverse values of worldliness. His denunciations of materialism naturally employ contrasts between abstract and concrete. A sense of the oppressiveness of material goods emerges in this accusation of Meed, with its picture of jewels and florins physically impeding the operation of law and faith:

> By Iesus! wiþ hire Ieweles youre Iustices she shendeþ
> And liþ ayein þe lawe and letteþ hym þe gate
> That feiþ may noȝt haue his forþ, hire floryns go so þikke.
>
> III 155–7

These images of the destruction of justice and the imprisonment of faith by Meed, the blockade of virtuous abstractions by concrete temptations, are strongly supported elsewhere in the poem: in attacks on the abuse of law, which I shall discuss in this chapter; in the initial description of Meed's sumptuous gems and clothing (II 8–17) in contrast with the plain linen (I 3) of Holy Church like a picture of sacred and profane love; in the Samaritan's prophecy of a redeemed society where faith would be the forester, walking freely and giving men the directions to Jerusalem (XVII 115–7).

Langland is fond of sets of alliterating words which emphasise the conflict of material and spiritual values. In Wit's discussion of marriage, he advises: 'For no londes, but for loue, loke ye be wedded' (IX 180). Wit uses, in C, a complex series of words which sound alike or are even identical, in form or root if not in meaning, to describe the short-sightedness of those who choose this world rather than the next:

> . . . thei loueþ and by-leyueþ al here lyf-tyme
> More in catel þan in kynde þat alle kyne þynges wroghte,
> The whiche is boþe loue and lyf and lasteþ withouten ende.
>
> C XI 167–9

People not only love the transient world of appearance during their lifetimes but even believe in it, mistake it for reality. Their love is directed to the mutable rather than to divine love and eternal life. They place faith in the created rather than the Creator, 'Kynde' who made every 'kind' of thing. The Dreamer, also, as I shall show later, traps himself in the ambiguities of the word 'kind', but in a mistaken approach to understanding rather than out of greed for material gain. As well as exploiting the various meanings of 'kind', Langland plays with the relationships between 'God' and 'good', moral 'goodness' and worldly 'goods'. 'Moore to good þan to god þe gome his loue caste,' (XIII 356) and 'Of þe good pat þow hem gyuest *ingrati* ben manye;/Ac god, of þi goodnesse gyue hem grace to amende' (XIV 169–70) are only two examples of a criticism frequently made in this way.

Even in their religious practices and experience many Christians confuse 'goods' with 'good'. Both clergy and laity traffic in the spiritual or place excessive trust in the material. The Pardoner of the Prologue deceives the foolish with outward gestures and appurtenances:

> Lewed men leued hym wel and liked his speche;
> Comen vp knelynge to kissen his bulle.
> He bonched hem with his breuet and blered hire eiȝen
> And rauȝte with his Rageman rynges and broches.
>
> Prol. 72–5

Similarly, the palmer of Passus V, who has never heard of Truth, sports all the visible signs of pilgrimage: 'a burdoun', 'a bolle and a bagge', 'an hundred of Ampulles', 'Signes of Synay and shelles of Galice,/And many crouch on his cloke and keyes of Rome,/And þe vernycle bifore,' (V 517–23). In both cases the physical details convey superstition, a dependence on talismanic possessions or compulsive ritual as a surrogate for spiritual experience. Hawkin's complaint that the Popes can no longer perform miracles as the apostles did shows that he desires corporal rather than spiritual blessings from the Church. The crudity of his view of the apostolic succession is exposed in his concrete language: 'For siþ he haþ þe power þat Peter hadde he haþ þe pot wiþ þe salue' (XIII 254). Yet if material cupidity is described in dismissive concrete vocabulary, spiritual acquisitiveness sounds more gross than acceptance of Meed or lust for miracles. All Langland's disgust at gluttony and misuse of riches informs his description of the spiritual sin of the dabblers in theological speculation who 'dryuele at hir deys þe deitee to knowe,/And gnawen god in þe gorge whanne hir guttes fullen' (X 57–8).

Langland's discussions of legal practice usually suggest that justice resides only in the ideal and is corrupted in the application of the law. In the Prologue lawyers are introduced thus:

> Yet houed þer an hundred in howues of selk,
> Sergeantȝ it semed þat serueden at þe barre,
> Pleteden for penyes and pounded þe lawe

Ac noʒt for loue of oure lord vnlose hire lippes ones.
Prol. 211–14

We reserve judgement over the first concrete detail of the
silk hoods: they may be merely emblematic as a badge of
office but they may suggest that lawyers are in the business
for the money. The latter interpretation is supported by the
contrast of pounds and pence with the love of the Lord.[7] The
lawyers are exploiting for venal purposes the divine gifts of
speech and intelligence. The insubstantiality of their dedication to justice is cogently expressed in the next lines:

Thow myʒtest bettre meete myst on Maluerne hilles
Than gete a mom of hire mouþ til moneie be shewed.
Prol. 215–16

Theology orders that Meed be taken to London and the
legality of her proposed marriage with False be examined but
he shows little trust in the integrity of the professionals who
will judge the case. He invokes the abstract qualities which
judges should represent but doubts whether the 'justice' will
'judge' accordingly:

Wercheþ by wisdom and by wit after;
Ledeþ hire to Londoun þere lawe is yhandled,
If any lewte wol loke þei ligge togideres.
And if þe Iustice Iugge hire to be Ioyned wiþ Fals
Yet be war of þe weddynge; for witty is truþe,
For Conscience is of his counseil and knoweþ yow echone;
II 134–9

Law may be perverted by actual justices and Conscience has
to determine the relationship of personal motive and action
to the absolute, Truth. Only certain abstractions such as
Truth, Conscience, Wit and Wisdom are to be trusted – and,
in the same vision, 'wit' and 'wisdom' will prove to be very
ambiguous words. In Conscience's prophecy of the perfect
society, justice is administered by the abstraction and the
lawyers, together with the rewards of their profession, have
vanished:

And whoso trespaseþ to truþe or takeþ ayein his wille,
Leaute shal don hym lawe and no lif ellis.
Shal no sergeant for þat seruice were a silk howue,
Ne no pelure in his panelon for pledynge at þe barre;

III 293–6

The sense of the distance of human versions of justice from
their divine origin culminates in the same speech in a vision
of the bureaucratic divisions and sub-divisions of the law in
human society replaced by a single ideal relationship between the individual and authority, of the Many dissolved
into the One: 'Kynges Court and commune Court, Consis-
torie and Chapitle,/ Al shal be but oon court, and oon burn
be Iustice' (III 319–21). Most of Langland's descriptions of
lawyers and judicial procedure use concrete vocabulary to
suggest an adverse comparison with such abstractions as
Justice and Truth. But Conscience's picture of the perfect
society includes this prediction: 'Ac kynde loue shal come 3it
and Conscience togideres/ And make of lawe a laborer;
swich loue shal arise . . .' (III 299–300), and Reason, in his
similar prophecy, uses the same phrase: 'That lawe shal ben
a laborer and lede afeld donge,' (IV 147). When the state has
withered away, there will be no call for law: at one level,
lawyers will have to become labourers and do some honest
work at last; at another level, there will be no need for the
abstract word for law because each actual man will embody
the ideal.

Langland sometimes yokes an abstract and a concrete
word together in such a combination as 'Mesure is medicine'
(I 35). This terse equation suggests, in form as well as in
content, the power of the spirit over the body. Measure is
medicine because, paradoxically, it is not medicine: it is
prevention rather than cure. In this case the abstract word
dominates the concrete so completely that the latter is given
a negative value. Other ironic juxtapositions are 'Siþ charite
haþ ben chapman' (Prol. 64) and 'now is Religion a rydere' (X
311). These expressions insist that the ideal is imperfectly
realised in the world or is even perverted into something
evil. But the movement from abstract to concrete may also
suggest the converse, that evil qualities should be converted
into positive moral action in the world of material need:

Reason cannot show pity for malefactors until, among other improvements in society, 'clerkene coueitise be to cloþe þe pouere and fede' (IV 119). In his last dissipated fling in Passus XX, Life both misinterprets virtue and belittles it by scaling it down from abstract to concrete terms: 'And heeld holynesse a Iape and hendenesse a wastour' (XX 145).[8] The same verbal strategy, however, can expose the sham appearance of virtue, so that 'harlottes holynesse be holden for an heþyng' (IV 118). While the movement from abstract to concrete in 'charite . . . chapman' suggests a contemptuous and disillusioned view of the operations of charity in the world, the same technique can as easily assert the vigour and practicality of the ideal:

> . . . dedly synne doþ he noȝt for dowel hym helpeþ,
> That is charite þe champion, chief help ayein synne.
>
> VIII 44–5

Piers accounts for his miraculous gift of learning in a structurally similar formulation: 'Abstinence þe Abbesse myn a b c me tauȝte' (VII 138), confronting the officious priest with the view that God can work as effectively through individual virtue as through ecclesiastical institutions.

Perhaps the most moving example in *Piers* of contrast between abstract and concrete is a line whose drift is towards tolerance rather than satire. In Passus XVIII, when Christ's entry into Jerusalem is described as the approach of a knight to be dubbed and to fight his first tournament, the Dreamer asks Faith who will be the adversary:

> 'Who shal Iuste wiþ Iesus,' quod I, 'Iewes or Scrybes?'
> 'Nay,' quod feiþ, 'but þe fend and fals doom to deye.
> Deeþ seiþ he shal fordo and adoun brynge
> Al þat lyueþ or lokeþ in londe or in watre.
> Lif seiþ þat he lieþ . . .'
>
> XVIII 27–31

Faith's answer does not confirm the prejudice latent in the Dreamer's question and the form of question and answer provides a commentary on each. The Dreamer's 'Jews or scribes?' pre-supposes an answer in its own simple concrete terms but Faith replies in a series of abstractions which become increasingly difficult to visualise. The 'fend' suggests the Devil and all his influence, the evil in all men, not merely Jews and scribes; 'fals doom' is, locally, the decision of Pilate but, generally, all the perversions of justice and judgement which Langland has shown as endemic to individual and society; Death, the universal conqueror to whom all humans submit, is challenged by the source of life. Faith's 'Nay' contradicts the Dreamer directly but the form of his answer is an implicit criticism of the question. It suggests that the person who is incapable of thinking abstractly is particularly prone to mistaken judgements, 'fals doom'. He sees only what happens and not the meaning of what happens. Therefore, when he sees the Jews apparently causing the death of Jesus, he falls unthinkingly into a harmful anti-semitic interpretation. The true causes – the Fall, man's sin and error, God's promise of eternal life – are hidden from the man who judges by appearances.

Much of my discussion has suggested that, while Langland makes heavy use of personified abstractions and finds the world of sense data handy for pointing a moral, his use of concrete vocabulary is frequently derogatory. The writer of religious allegory stands in a complex relationship to the material world: he tacitly admits that he needs it to embody concept, to move, persuade, attract, repel, explain; but his major practice is to replace the fallen world with a more spiritual and coherent one. Yet the orthodox Christian view is not that matter and the body are intrinsically evil: God saw at the creation of the world that it was good; the body is to be resurrected; the Incarnation dignifies human life.

Some of Langland's expressions – for example 'lawe shal ben a laborer' – suggest a respect for the concrete and human and its capacity to embody the ideal. In C *Liberum Arbitrium* insists to Will, who characteristically wants to make a precise but misleading distinction, in an image anticipating the Samaritan's metaphor of the indivisible Trinity as wax, wick and flame, that body and soul are interdependent:

'[I] may nat be with-oute a body to bere me wher hym

lykeþ.'
'Thenne is þat body bettere þan þow,' quaþ ich, 'nay,'
   quaþ he, 'no betere
Bote as a wode were a fure þenne worchen þei boþe,
And ayþer is oþeres heete and also of a wil
And so is man þat haþ hus mynde myd *Liberum arbitrium*.'

C XVII 178–82

As body and soul are bound in a subtle knot and need each
other, so the Holy Spirit urgently breaks through the barriers
between heaven and earth and throws itself into human
hands:

. . . þe heiȝe holy goost heuene shall tocleue,
And loue shal lepen out after into þis lowe erþe,
And clennesse shal cacchen it and clerkes shullen it fynde:

XII 139–41

Heaven is high, earth low, but, in a violent metaphor, the
Spirit 'cleaves' perfection so that love can 'leap' to be
available to the abstraction 'purity' and the particular
'clerks'. The metaphorical complex in which Holy Church
describes the Incarnation as the 'plante of pees' (I 152)[9]
proceeds through a swift series of intricately contrasting and
conciliating vocabulary: love is too 'hevy' for 'hevene' but,
paradoxically, when it has taken 'flessh & blood' and is
compounded with 'erþe', is the most 'light' thing in the
world; it feels tangibly 'portatif' and 'persaunt'; it is as sharp
as the 'point of a nedle' but, like a geometrical point, has no
dimension; no physical defences, 'Armure' or 'heiȝe walles',
are proof against its subtle power. It would be perverse – or
impossible – to chart the abstract and concrete associations
of the imagery: the passage achieves a brilliant synthesis of
the material and the spiritual, the earthly and the heavenly.
   In Passus XVII the Samaritan, representing Christ,
recommends trust neither in earthly remedies nor in abstract
virtue but in a sacramentalism which unites the physical and
spiritual worlds:

May no medicyne vnder mone þe man to heele brynge,
Neiþer Feiþ ne fyn hope, so festred be hise woundes,

Wiþouten þe blood of a barn . . .'

XVII 94–6

He goes on to affirm that, in his battle with the powers of evil, his humanity gives him a strength which Faith and Hope lack:

> For an Outlawe is in þe wode and vnder bank lotieþ,
> And may ech man see and good mark take
> Who is bihynde and who bifore and who ben on horse;
> For he halt hym hardier on horse þan he þat is on foote.
> For he seigh me þat am Samaritan suwen Feiþ and his
> felawe
> On my Capul þat highte *caro* – of mankynde I took it –
> He was vnhardy, þat harlot, and hidde hym *in Inferno*.

XVII 105–11

The importance placed on the human makes this a particularly gentle allegory of the Atonement. Christ defends man through a relationship of mutual courtesy: man lent him the horse, '*caro*'. The fears the Dreamer expressed earlier for those who lived 'bifore' the coming of Christ are allayed in the verb 'suwen': Abraham and Moses wait, the Faith and Hope of the Old Testament expect fulfilment and it does follow.

Christ, the Samaritan, Charity and Piers are fused in the symbolism of this vision. But the role of Piers as the human nature of Christ is carefully distinguished. At the beginning of Passus XVIII Will sees the resemblance between Piers, the Samaritan and the one who rides into Jerusalem and asks Faith if Piers is there. Faith replies:

> This Iesus of his gentries wol Iuste in Piers armes,
> In his helm and in his haubergeon, *humana natura*;
> That crist be no3t yknowe here for *consummatus deus*
> In Piers paltok þe Plowman þis prikiere shal ryde,
> For no dynt shal hym dere as *in deitate patris*.

XVIII 22–6

Faith identifies the figure Will sees as perfect God and perfect man, unifying and balancing abstract and concrete in his description. Jesus, in his 'gentries' and *'deitas'*, will employ the 'armes', 'helm' and 'haubergeon' of Piers. These, like the horse *'caro'*, give God potency to intervene visibly in the sinful world of fallen humanity. But the humility, as well as the power, of the Incarnation is emphasised by a shift in the imagery. Piers, increasingly associated in the *Vita* with divine wisdom, entered the *Visio* as a simple industrious ploughman. And at the triumphal moment of the entry into Jerusalem we are reminded of this role; Christ rides in his 'paltok'. The ploughman's garment, symbol of the physical labour of the least pretentious human beings, momentarily displaces the more glamorous metaphor of the knight's armour and becomes the other nature of the abstract impassible Latinate divinity.

Faith, here, and Conscience in the next passus (XIX 10–14) expound clearly the allegory of Piers as the human nature of Christ. I should like to suggest tentatively that this relationship may provide the clue to a problematic passage which, as far as I know, has never been satisfactorily explained. In the account of the life of Christ in the inner vision in Passus XVI Piers is said to teach the growing Jesus:

> And in þe wombe of þat wenche was he fourty woukes
> Til he weex a faunt þoruȝ hir flessh and of fightyng kouþe
> To haue yfouȝte wiþ þe fend er ful tyme come.
> And Piers þe Plowman parceyued plener tyme
> And lered hym lechecraft his lif for to saue
> That, þouȝ he were wounded with his enemy, to waris-
> shen hymselue;
> And dide hym assaie his surgenrie on hem þat sike were
> Til he was parfit praktisour . . .
>
> XVI 100–7

There is evidence that some medieval theologians believed that Christ, being divine, always had perfect knowledge. Medieval paintings depicting Jesus learning to read were condemned as heterodox.[10] St. Luke's gospel relates how the doctors in the temple were amazed at the understanding of the twelve year old child (*Luke* II 46, 47). Yet it is emotionally difficult to reconcile the unnatural and rather exasperating idea of an omniscient infant with a sense of the full humanity of Christ. Perhaps Langland in this passage tactfully attempts a resolution consistent with the claims of orthodoxy: Christ is shown as learning in connection with Piers, his human nature.[11] The obvious objection to this interpretation is that we might expect Piers to be the learner rather than the teacher. Perhaps this difficulty is resolved if we consider human learning, in contrast to divine intuition, as a patient process of subjection to time. (Will is accused, in A, of resenting the fact: 'Þe were lef to lerne but loþ for to stodie' (A XII 6).) In Passus XIX of C, where *Liberum Arbitrium* replaces Piers, the equivalent passage opens thus:

> And in þe wombe of þat wenche he was fourty wokes,
> And man by-cam of þat mayde to saue mankynde,
> Byg and abydynge and bold in his barn-hede,
> To hauen fouhten with þe feende ar ful tyme come.
> Ac *liberum arbitrium* leche-crafte hym tauhte,
> Til plenitudo temporis hih tyme approchede,
> That suche a surgeyn setthen yseye was þer neuere,
> Ne non so faithfol fysicien . . .

> C XIX 134–41

In this revision as much emphasis is placed upon the theme of *plenitudo temporis* as on that of leechcraft. God's will could be effected instantaneously but, as Reason puts it to the Dreamer in Passus XI: 'He myȝte amende in a Minute while al þat mysstandeþ,/ Ac he suffreþ for som mannes goode . . .' (XI 381–2). Divine power permits itself to be restrained by the humanity of Piers (or *Liberum Arbitrium*) and harnessed to its tempo; Being submits to Becoming.

The interplay between abstract and concrete words is full of potential for Langland as Christian poet and allegorist. Through it he can both condemn materialism and give audience to the claims of the body, demonstrate the importance and difficulty of abstract thought, make manifest the spiritual and create literary structures which act as parables of the doctrine of Incarnation. Yet he also presents this interplay as hazardous, as a possible basis for constructing false patterns which distort and impede understanding.

A type of question sometimes asked in *Piers Plowman* is one where the naïvety of the speaker is exposed not only by the enquiry itself but also in the choice of words. The self-incrimination of the foolish questioner is evident in the Dreamer's 'What kynnes þyng is kynde?' (IX 25). The play on the two meanings of 'kynde' ('sort' and 'God') highlights Will's misunderstanding: he is trying to limit the creator ('kynde'), source of nature ('kynde'), to being one sort ('kynne') of creature, unable to grasp the idea of the One as he ferrets among the Many. Wit instructs him both by explaining what 'kynde' is and by using the word in its different senses correctly: 'Kynde . . . is a creatour of alle kynnes beestes' (IX 26).

A similar obtuseness emerges in Hawkin's 'Where wonyeþ Charite?' (XIV 98) and in the Dreamer's attempts to find a person called Dowel:

. . . I romed aboute
Al a somer seson for to seke dowel,
And frayned ful ofte of folk þat I mette
If any wi3t wiste wher dowel was at Inne;
And what man he my3te be of many man I asked.

VIII 1–5

The confusion in thinking Dowel a man is emphasised in the repetition of the word 'man', used by Will both for the actual persons he asks and for the abstraction he seeks, and imitated mockingly by Thought:

Wher dowel and dobet and dobest ben in londe
Here is wil wolde wite if wit koude hym teche;
And wheiþer he be man or no man þis man wolde aspie
. . .'

VIII 128–30

It is obvious that an irony plays over the search for Dowel and that the Dreamer is to some extent making the mistake that sends people on pilgrimages or persuades them to trust the gewgaws of the Pardoner or deceives them into trying to atone for their sins by financing stained glass windows (III 60–75): he is over-valuing the concrete.

The concrete form of the Dreamer's enquiries about Dowel and of Hawkin's about Charity is clearly incongruous. Yet why are these questions so inappropriate in an allegorical poem? They are, after all, answered in the same style. Thought seemed to mock the crudity of Will's image of Dowel but Wit does not scruple to reply that Dowel lives in a castle made by Kynde (IX 1–24). When Hawkin asks where Charity dwells, he is first answered in abstractions: 'Ther parfit truþe and poore herte is, and pacience of tonge . . .' (XIV 100). But in the next passus Anima is content to describe Charity in concrete terms: he comes often into the king's court but seldom into the consistory (XV 235, 239); he has been seen both in rags and rich robes and, a long time ago, in a friar's habit (XV 225–32); when he is tired of pilgrimages and such acts of mercy as visiting prisoners, he works in a laundry (XV 182–92). We are expected to understand at once that the work in the laundry symbolises the cleansing of the soul by penitence and not accuse Anima of imagining that Charity is one actual person. So it is not necessarily mistaken to use concrete terms to describe virtues or spiritual conditions. Langland seems to be having it both ways. He is both employing and sabotaging the potentialities for concreteness in the allegorical mode. Wit is allowed to describe the Castle of Kynde in reply to the question 'Where does Dowel live?' but the Dreamer is a literal-minded fool for asking such a question.[12]

The double use of allegory in these examples, as both misleading habit of thought and vehicle for genuine insight, seems to me symptomatic of Langland's simultaneously respectful and suspicious attitude towards the mode. In the last chapters I shall discuss the problems Langland found in allegory and the ways in which he dealt with them.

# 5 Objections to Allegory: Allegory as Prejudice

Langland suggests that the Dreamer is wrong to ask where Dowel lives but that Wit is right to reply with the allegorical picture of the Castle of Kynde. So the validity of an allegory depends upon its being properly understood. Dr. Johnson's complaint about the figures of Fame and Victory was that such personifications were inert and predictable, all too easily understood and exhausted. An hypostatisation of Victory by definition wins a cheap victory because there is nothing else it can do. Langland's allegory surely raises too many problems of interpretation for it to be accused, in general, of being boringly obvious. Nevertheless, there are some moments at which I find it specious and mechanical. But these are exceptional. I want in this chapter to argue that Langland's allegory is an enquiring form. It should be seen in the context of a vital cosmology of God-given analogies. Langland used it for purposes of exploration and definition. He was employing a form which was traditionally thought not obvious, but arcane.

For most of the Dowel section Will's quest for understanding takes the form of conversations with various abstractions, aspects of intelligence and wisdom. These characters represent, to a greater or lesser degree, aspects of the Dreamer himself. While Study seems to stand for all secular and Clergy for all sacred learning, Thought resembles the narrator, expects to be recognised and has followed him for the traditional long epoch of seven years (VIII 70–5). Ranged along a continuum from the more general to the more particular, these characters have all much the same kind of relationship to the enquiring narrator. The classic and influential figure of Philosophy in the *Consolation* of Boethius shows how the polarities of general and particular may be united in one hypostatisation: she is both the Idea of all human philosophy and what Boethius exiled and alone in prison, without books, restricting himself to the deductions of human reason, not availing himself of the Christian revelation, can salvage from his own intelligence and his lifetime of study.[1] Langland's Dreamer shows less capacity than Boethius to profit from his inner debate. Perhaps it is too inward and theoretical, contradicting in its very form the monition that echoes, variously expressed, throughout *Piers Plowman*: 'And þe moore þat a man of good matere hereþ,/But he do þerafter, it dooþ hym double scaþe.' (XV 58–9). When we emphasise the authority of the abstractions, Will's attempt to turn a vertical into a horizontal debate looks perverse and rebellious. When we respond to them as 'properties' of the Dreamer, the debate itself can seem circular and claustrophobic.

It is therefore a turning-point when, in the inner dream in Passus XI, Will looks out of himself and is shown the vision of Middle Earth. After all the tergiversations of the inner quarrel, its infuriating propensity to obsession and digression, the arrival of Kynde offers release and objectivity:

> This lokynge on lewed preestes haþ doon me lepe from pouerte
> The which I preise, þer pacience is, moore parfit þan richesse.
> Ac muche moore in metynge þus wiþ me gan oon dispute,
> And slepynge I sei3 al þis, and siþen cam kynde
> And nempned me by my name and bad me nymen hede,
> And þoru3 þe wondres of þis world wit for to take.
> And on a mountaigne þat myddelerþe hi3te, as me þo þou3te,
> I was fet forþ by forbisenes to knowe
> Thorugh ech a creature kynde my creatour to louye.
>
> XI 318–26

The account of nature which follows is one of the most readily attractive passages in *Piers Plowman*. It is easy to share the Dreamer's awe at the 'wondres' and beauty of the world and at the precision with which nature works. Birds, for example, mysteriously know how to build nests so intricate that no trained mason could reproduce them (XI 345–50). Yet Will is, characteristically, irritated as well as impressed: why should man, he demands of Reason, be apparently the least rational of God's creatures (XI 369–75)? Reason refuses to answer 'reasonably'. He poses instead another question, 'Who suffreþ moore þan god?' (XI 380), and suggests that the example of divine suffering might inspire Will to tolerate more and to criticise less (XI 387–404). Will wakes from the inner dream distressed that he has not learnt more from it. His shame makes him responsive to his next mentor, Imaginatif, who is quick to point out that Will forfeited the opportunity to learn more by his interruption. He has repeated Adam's original sin of vain curiosity (XI 417–19). Imaginatif tells him 'þow contrariedest clergie wiþ crabbede wordes' and 'aresonedest Reson' (XII, 156, 218), and at last Will seems ready to submit: 'Why ye wisse me þus,' quod I, 'was for I rebuked Reson.' (XI 438).

Imaginatif addresses himself in Passus XII to Will's major problems. He questions the value of the poem, offers a definition of Dowel and defends learning against the Dreamer's attacks on it. Turning to the most alarming problem, that of salvation, Imaginatif warns that not all mysteries can be penetrated by the human intelligence. Nevertheless he answers the queries about the cases of Trajan and the penitent thief and even holds out hope of universal salvation. 'Ac god is so good' (XII 272) that Imaginatif is optimistic about the fate of the virtuous pagans.

The meeting with Imaginatif is crucial to the Dreamer. After it, although he will always be subject to the same intellectual and moral temptations, he can proceed. In the next passus, when Conscience calls him to the banquet, we see how his attitude to learning has changed: 'And for Conscience of Clergie spak I com wel þe raþer.' (XIII 24). Yet, while Imaginatif's counsel is necessary, his dialectic can seem ludicrous, if not dishonest. In his defence of Clergy he asks Will this question:

Tak two stronge men and in Themese cast hem,
And boþe naked as a nedle, hir noon sadder þan ooþer,
That oon kan konnynge and kan swymmen and dyuen;
That ooþer is lewed of þat labour, lerned neuere swymme.
Which trowestow of þo two in Themese is in moost drede,
He þat neuere ne dyued ne noȝt kan of swymmyng,
Or þe swymmere þat is saaf by so hymself like,
Ther his felawe fleteþ forþ as þe flood likeþ
And is in drede to drenche, þat neuere dide swymme?

XII 160–8

Will replies: 'That swymme kan noȝt . . .' (XII 169). What else could he say? Imaginatif has put the question in a form which predetermines its answer, has indeed answered it himself several times in the course of posing it. He goes on to argue, triumphantly, by analogy that the learned are spiritually in a safer position than the ignorant. His 'proof' irritates, both by its smug Sunday School tone and by the shakiness of its reasoning. Use of analogy now seems respectable only to illustrate and clarify, not to prove or refute. Melville's criticism of the practice – 'You pun with ideas' – seems apt here.

Argument by analogy was deemed more proper in Langland's period than now. It was consonant with the major doctrines of medieval Christianity. The creation of man in God's image is an analogy: man's duty is to make it a convincing one.[2] The Incarnation and the opportunity it gave to imitate Christ confirm the potential likeness between God and man. The relationship between Christ and His Church should be echoed in society by king and subjects and in marriage by husband and wife. The events of the Old Testament foreshadow those of the New: God's allegory deals in 'facts' as well as 'words'.[3] The whole world, indeed, was conceived as a book written by God, hierarchically ordered and full of edifying correspondences, in which man could and should find meaning.[4]

The introduction to the vision of Middle Earth evokes such a cosmology. It suggests the relationships to be discovered between God, man and Nature. The word 'kynde' mediates between them, denoting both God (XI 321) and his works (XI 326), and standing significantly between the words 'creature' and 'creatour' (XI 326). God calls the Dreamer by his name, as Adam, in his turn, named the animals. The impression of unfallen nature in this vision is so strong that the world looks newly created, with man as the only discordant element. The Dreamer may be theologically imprecise in ascribing the possession of 'Reason' to animals but he is right to see that they bear witness to the *logos* which created them. Nature is felt to be irresistibly instructive: it will, in every detail, teach the Dreamer to love its maker. He will learn from its examples (XI 325). Later, in *As You Like It*, Shakespeare's Duke will see sermons in stones more easily in his harsh rustic exile, but for the medieval poet they are everywhere. The *exempla* in medieval sermons often seem crudely moralistic, designed to appeal to the most childish credulity, but the use of 'example' here shows the sense of imaginative connection between the homilist's improving anecdotes and the intelligible coherence of God's universe. It is in this intellectual context that Imaginatif's two strong men respectively sink and swim. Imaginatif sees his analogical arguments as limited but not fallacious. They are a just exercise of human reasoning but not all problems can be solved by human reason. Yet, although grace is superior, both clergy and 'kynde wit' are desirable (XII 64–70). Clergy, the reading and writing of books, is an analogue of divine activity: 'Alþouȝ men made bokes þe maister was god,/And seint Spirit þe Samplarie, and seide what men sholde write' (XII 101–2). The Holy Spirit provides yet another aspect of 'example'. And the Book of Nature is available to all men. Kynde Wit, the knowledge that comes from what we see (XII 67), can afford instructions for pagans as well as Christians: 'Ac of briddes and of beestes men by olde tyme/Ensamples token and termes, as telleþ þise poetes' (XII 236–7). Nature yields analogies as gratifying as the comparison of the glorious peacock, who can neither fly nor sing well, to the rich man and his gaudy encumbrances (XII 236–63).

There is divine use of analogy, inspiration for the preacher's *exempla* and the religious poet's metaphors, similes and allegories. Imaginatif both expounds and illustrates this view. But how far would Langland have been aware that analogy could mislead, could be used in a bad cause? Chaucer's Parson could expose a false analogy. In *The*

*Merchant's Tale* January implies to May that within marriage any kind of sexual activity is lawful: 'A man may do no synne with his wyf,/ Ne hurte hymselven with his owene knyf' (*CT*, IV 1839–40). The Parson retorts in his discussion of lechery: 'And for that many man weneth that he may nat synne, for no likerousnesse that he dooth with his wyf, certes, that opinion is false. God woot, a man may sleen hymself with his owene knyf . . .' (*CT* X 855). Yet his own use of argument by analogy can seem grotesque, even allowing for the correspondences seen between the various realms of nature: '. . . it was ordeyned that o man sholde have but o womman, and o womman but o man . . . a man is heved of a womman; algate, by ordnaunce it sholde be so. For if a womman hadde mo men than oon, thanne sholde she have moo hevedes than oon, and that were an horrible thyng biforn God . . .' (*CT* X 920). He is implicitly rebuking the Wife of Bath's defiance on the subjects of monogamy and masculine supremacy; one suspects, however, that she will be immune to this strategy. She has already proved herself adept at turning the arguments of authority 'up-so-doun'. In her Prologue she leaves without comment an 'example' which has not persuaded her to imitate it: she has been told

> That sith that Crist ne wente nevere but onis
> To weddyng, in the Cane of Galilee,
> That by the same ensample taughte he me
> That I ne sholde wedded be but ones.

*CT* III 10–13

Is the Wife of Bath unable to refute this argument or does she not think it worth refuting? I think that she implicitly scorns it: lack of comment in Chaucer usually produces an effect of scepticism and the Wife, elsewhere in her Prologue, is a loquacious and resourceful sophist in defending her unorthodox position. I find that the contrast between the remote 'Cane of Galilee' and the immediate 'taughte he me' suggests that this analogy is far-fetched, that there is an unjustifiable gulf here between 'authority' and 'experience'. One could 'prove' anything by such random application of 'example'. The theory that in God's work deeds can be as allegorical as words has resulted in punning with facts.

Langland seems aware of the possibility of being deceived by false analogy when, in Passus XVII, Will tries to choose between the commandments of Faith and Hope. Faith has told him to believe in the Trinity; Hope has told him to love God and his neighbour. Instead of accepting the counsels of both, the Dreamer dismisses Hope, who appears to demand more, quantitatively and qualitatively, than Faith:

'The gome þat gooþ wiþ o staf, he semeþ in gretter heele
Than he þat gooþ wiþ two staues to sighte of vs alle;
And riȝt so, bi þe roode, Reson me sheweþ
It is lighter to lewed men o lesson to knowe
Than for to techen hem two, and to hard to lerne þe leeste!
It is ful hard for any man on Abraham bileue
And wel awey worse ȝit for to loue a sherewe.
It is lighter to leeue in þre louely persones
Than for to louye and lene as wel lorels as lele.
Go þi gate!'quod I to *Spes*, 'so me god helpe,
Tho þat lernen þi lawe wol litel while vsen it.'

XVII 39–49

It is clear that Will's Either/Or approach is mistaken, despite his confident appeal to 'Reson', and when, later in the passus, he puts the dilemma to the Samaritan, he is told to follow the teachings of both Faith and Hope (XVII 127–37). It is easy enough to explain why the analogy is false. In the Christian scheme man is spiritually sick and in need of as much support as possible so that two 'staues' are better than one. Learning has been proved conducive to salvation so that two lessons may be more profitable than one. Yet Hope does not point out the fallacies in Will's attack on him. The problem is solved by the authority (not arguments) of the Samaritan. Does Hope think Will not worth the compliment of rational opposition? Will is rude ('Go þi gate') as well as obstinate and Hope may be wise not to argue his case with such an unreceptive audience. He is vindicated by the Samaritan whom Will immediately respects: he asks to be his 'gome' (XVII 88), thanks him for his friendship (XVII 90) and addresses him as 'swete sire' (XVII 127) when he requests advice on the commandments of Faith and Hope. Or does Langland know that there is something wrong in his narrator's procedure in rebutting Hope but himself lack the concept of false analogy with which to analyse it? Although elsewhere in the poem allegorical characters are quick to rebuke the narrator, I think this explanation unlikely. There seems no reason to suppose Langland blinder to this kind of fallacious reasoning than Chaucer's Parson. Perhaps the answer is suggested in the C revision of the passage.[5] Here the poet re-phrases Will's speech, at some cost to both vividness and coherence, and deletes the analogies, as if he feared that the audience might be misled by the false conclusions of the Dreamer. I suspect that Langland felt analogy to be seductive, so appealing to the intellect that it had better not be used in a bad cause.

An allegorical poet may be expected to respond to the appeal of analogy. Moral allegory is a form of argument by analogy. It too provides for the receptive a sense that the world is orderly, that ethical and spiritual values can be demonstrated. But it can provoke similar objections from the unsympathetic. It may seem to preach to the converted, to persuade only those who already share but enjoy rein-forcement of its views. Its conclusions may seem unfounded, its tone sanctimonious. It raises the same prob-lems of aptness of metaphor. And, curiously, an appropriate 'figure' provokes almost the same suspicions as an incon-gruous one. When an analogy seems false, we feel that the case has not been proved but that the author is assuming its justice.[6] But if the analogy rings absolutely true, the proceed-ings may look unnecessary. Allegory can seem tautological, as though the description and actions of an allegorical personage were only an extension of his name, like a definition in a dictionary. And the judgement passed upon him may seem equally inevitable. Gluttony eats, drinks, vomits, grows fat; he is a sin and the author is against him. A traditional allegorical form, the psychomachia, may seem to rig the battle before it begins: how can anyone (except a decadent) be for the vices and against the virtues when they are so unambiguously labelled? Like Imaginatif's example of the two men in the Thames, all seems pre-determined, not exploratory.

But did Langland mean his poem to be an exploration? Would he have considered poetry a means of discovery or fresh enquiry a merit in poetry? He would probably have been surprised at the attention paid to this question in modern literary theory. He might well have thought almost blasphemous the claims made for the importance of poetry in such a formulation as this by R. P. Blackmur: 'Poetry is like mathematics, morals like physics; and it is sometimes "true" that poetry creates the morals in the same sense that poetry creates the felt relations of things, which unite the substance and the problems of morals . . . Poetry takes action in morals as mathematics does in physics.'[7] The idea here that poetry precedes or determines morals is almost the opposite of the medieval theory. For Langland the Christian poet already lives in a world of revealed doctrine and morality. Whereas Angus Fletcher thinks allegory prone to omit the 'human detail', vexing and protean material for 'the felt relations of things, which unite the substance and the problems of morals', Langland probably saw in allegory opportunity for the dramatisation of known truths. My distinction between proof and illustration by analogy is redundant where proof is not required.

Certainly the conviction that truth is readily available runs through *Piers Plowman* from Holy Church's insistence in Passus I on innate knowledge to Kynde's final repetition in Passus XX of the central Christian command, 'Lerne to loue' (XX 208). Yet the truths of Christianity, revealed and believed, seem inaccessible and the poem an attempt to apprehend them. Imaginatif tries to dismiss *Piers* as unnecessary since other books and other people already expound Dowel, Dobet and Dobest. Will, however, insists that he cannot abandon the poem unless someone can explain these terms to his satisfaction. In one sense he believes and understands the teachings of Christianity; in another he must 'realise' them for himself. Langland is acutely conscious of the need to 'unite the substance and the problems of morals'. In later chapters I shall discuss his suspicion that the allegorical mode may play down this need by idealising and spiritualising the human world of compromise and contingency. Here I want to show how his allegory confronts the problem of tautology and avoids simple equations between instances and absolutes.

Far from using allegory tautologically, Langland sees one

of its functions as definition. This can be illustrated most easily from the episode of Meed, which stresses that names cannot be taken on trust but invite one to examine a variety of concepts. For example, the characters Wisdom and Witty follow Reason to London when he goes to advise the King:

> . . . for þei hadde to doone
> In cheker and in Chauncerye, to ben descharged of þynges.
> And riden faste for Reson sholde rede hem þe beste
> For to saue hemseluen from shame and from harmes.
>
> IV 28–31

Their names initially disarm the audience – Theology has already recommended the exercise of 'wisdom' and 'wit' in the decision about Meed's marriage (II 134) – but they are evil characters, representing the abuse of the qualities they are named for.[8] Aspects of wordly wisdom, they wish to bribe Reason to help them in dishonest transactions and later in the passus (IV 67–82) they use their ingenuity in an attempt to have Wrong acquitted. Meed herself has the most alarmingly (but illuminatingly) polysemous name: the stability of the kingdom and the just conduct of the individual depend upon a true appraisal of the various meanings of the word. Meed claims (III 209–227) to be the rightful munificence of a monarch and the just payment which men expect to give and to take in return for work. 'No wiȝt, as I wene, wiþouten Mede may libbe' (III 227), she concludes, and the King is temporarily convinced by her.

Conscience refutes her by distinguishing between the different senses of 'meed' and showing that she has been using the word improperly:

> 'Nay', quod Conscience to þe kyng and kneled to þe erþe.
> 'There are two manere of Medes, my lord, bi youre leue.
> That oon god of his grace gyueþ in his blisse
> To hem þat werchen wel while þei ben here.
> The prophete precheþ it and putte it in þe Sauter:
> *Domine, quis habitabit in tabernaculo tuo?*
> Lord, who shal wonye in þi wones wiþ þyne holy seintes,
> Or resten in þyne holy hilles: þis askeþ Dauid.

And Dauid assoileþ it hymself as þe Sauter telleþ
*Qui ingreditur sine macula & operatur Iusticiam.*
Tho þat entren of o colour and of one wille
And han ywroght werkes wiþ right and wiþ reson,
And he þat vseþ noȝt þe lyf of vsurie,
And enformeþ pouere peple and pursueþ truþe:
*Qui pecuniam suam non dedit ad vsuram et munera super*
    *innocentem &c.*
And alle þat helpen þe Innocent and holden with þe
    riȝtfulle,
Wiþouten Mede doþ hem good and þe truþe helpeþ,
Swiche manere men, my lord, shul haue þis firste Mede
Of god at a gret nede whan þei gon hennes.
Ther is a Mede mesurelees þat maistres desireþ
To mayntene mysdoers Mede þei take;
And þerof seiþ þe Sauter in a Salmes ende:
*In quorum manibus iniquitates sunt; dextra eorum repleta est*
    *muneribus.*
And he þat gripeþ hir giftes, so me god helpe,
Shal abien it bittre or þe book lieþ.
Preestes and persons þat plesynge desireþ,
That taken Mede and moneie for masses þat þei syngeþ,
Shul haue Mede on þis molde þat Mathew hap graunted:
*Amen amen Receperunt mercedem suam.*
That laborers and lowe lewede folk taken of hire maistres
It is no manere Mede but a mesurable hire.
In marchaundise is no Mede, I may it wel auowe;
It is a permutacion apertly, a penyworþ for anoþer.'

III 230–58

Conscience distinguishes between a heavenly sense of the
word 'meed' and an evil earthly sense which is almost an
ironic version of the celestial one. They have in common that
they are 'mesurelees', in excess, unearned. The reward of
heaven cannot be merited, even by those 'þat werchen wel';
God gives it 'of his grace'. The corrupt defendant is the
earthly version of the unearned: extortion, bribery, graft,
simony, usury. In her list of the occupations which live
'honestly' by meed she lumps together the venal and the
deserving in the same category. Priests who accept gifts for
celebrating the mass certainly receive meed, the earthly kind

at the cost of the heavenly. But the term should not be
applied to the just payment given to the honest labourer: he
accepts 'mesurable hire'. In the C text Langland replaces
'measurable hire' with a new word, 'mercede' (C IV 292), as
though one should not need to resort to periphrasis for so
necessary a concept. Yet, as often in C, an improvement in
clarity is gained at some expense. The ambiguity of the term
'meed', its evident currency as a description of just payment,
has a thematic function in the B argument: it explains why
the King should be deceived by Meed; it dramatises the
difficulty of forming true convictions about morality from
words and names which may be used quite differently on
different occasions.

Even the learned abstraction, Theology, is subject to this
difficulty. He sounds too trusting about 'wisdom' and 'wit'
and falls headlong into the trap set by Meed's name. Instead
of recognising that Meed is innately false, he takes her to be
the measurable hire of which the labourer is worthy and
objects that her proposed marriage to False would dishonour
her:

> . . . God graunted to gyue Mede to truþe,
> And þow has gyuen hire to a gilour, now god gyue þee
>    sorwe!
> The text telleþ þee noȝt so, Truþe woot þe soþe,
> For *Dignus est operarius* his hire to haue . . .
>
> II 120–23

Why should a character to whom Christians look for guidance on moral issues make this mistake? I think it is
because Theology's concerns are so predominantly with the
spiritual. His sense of the greatness and reality of the
heavenly meed blinds him to the equivocations with which
the word is used on earth. An addition in the C version
supports this interpretation:

> Ich theologie þe tixt knowe and trewe dome witnesseþ,
> Pat laurens þe leuite lyggynge on þe gredire,
> Loked vp to oure lorde and a-loud seide,
> 'God, of þy grace, heuene gates opene,
> For ich, man, of þy mercy mede haue deserued!'

And sythþe man may an hey mede of god deserue,
Hit semeþ ful sothly ryght so on erthe
That Mede may be wedded to no man bote to treuthe . . .
                                        C III 129–36

And if this mistake emphasises the power of Meed's
ambiguity, it also forces the reader to attempt a limiting
definition of Theology. We should not slackly accept the
authority of his name and uncritically trust his judgement in
all matters.

Words, like human behaviour, pose problems of evalua-
tion. Langland's sense of how language can deviate produces the grammatical analogy added in C in which 'mede'
and 'mercede' are analysed as 'two manere relacions,/Rect
and indyrect' (C IV 335–6).[9] 'Mercede' resembles a correct
agreement between adjective and noun, 'meed' a mistake in
grammar. Grammar demands that noun and adjective
should agree in case, number and gender: 'mercede', like a
correct form, is always appropriate to the circumstances;
'meed' is an improper qualification, irregularly attaching
herself to unsuitable subjects. To Langland all vital relationships can be described in these terms. The analogy between
God and man is the basis of other 'agreements': '. . . and
god, þe grounde of al, a graciouse antecedent./And man is
relatif rect yf he be ryht trewe;/He acordeþ with cryst in
kynde, uerbum caro factum est' (C IV 356–8). Grammatical
'accordance' serves as image of the likeness between God
and man and of the true relationship between master and
labourer, father and son, husband and wife, king and
subjects. Right use of language is, therefore, both practically
and analogically demanded. Words should stand in orderly
and correct relationships to each other, both to be truthful in
themselves and because their proper behaviour provides a
paradigm for so much else. But they are not, as actually
used, always to be trusted. And their misuse is a travesty of
the deepest agreements and accordance. The randomness of
Meed's behaviour, economic corruption, can be likened to
grammatical waywardness or to sexual promiscuity. 'Mede
þe mayde' (III 1) is, Conscience proves, 'As commune as þe
Cartwey' (III 132) and the court finally calls her a whore (IV
166). Language is corruptible: words too easily form unsuit-

able 'relationships', can be used to make false statements. And the polysemous quality of most abstractions makes them dangerously adaptable. Langland's yearning for clarity speaks when Conscience, defining the heavenly meed, translates *'sine macula'* as 'of o colour and of one wille' (III 238). Sinlessness is momentarily viewed as consistency.

I have indicated the attraction of allegory to a mind which views the world as a pattern of intended analogies. Its value, in such a scheme, is to reveal meanings latent in the cosmos. The centrality for the Dreamer of the vision of Middle Earth and Imaginatif's exposition of it shows Langland's sympathy with this cosmology. A modern agnostic reader may object that such allegory pre-judges, mechanically repeats the great platitudes of its time, proceeds with a clarity made possible only by omission. But in the Meed episode Langland drama-tises the dangers of pre-judging: words cannot be taken on trust; concepts – Meed, Theology, Wisdom – must be seen in relation to particular circumstances; human language and actions are not clear but confusing. Analogy itself, the earthly Meed's metaphorical resemblance to the heavenly, can deceive and must be carefully scrutinised.

Traditionally, allegory did not seem a clear and simplistic mode of expression. Its etymology, 'speaking otherwise', suggested the opposite and it was valued for being both overt and mysterious. The figurative language of Scripture set an example of sacred obscurity. All human language about God must be metaphorical, approximate and 'accom-modated' but there is a spiritual advantage even in its inadequacy. It repels the superficial; it encourages the thoughtful to think profoundly. Expounding the text *'Penitet me fecisse eos* (*Genesis* 7 vii): It repenteth me that I have made them', Gregory warns that the analogy is necessary but imperfect: God, with absolute goodness and foreknowledge, could not change his mind but approximations such as *penitet* are not surprising *'si spirituales plerumque utantur verbis carnalium*: if the spiritual generally use the words of the carnal'. This, for Gregory, is an example of the way in which the Bible can be understood only by the receptive and initiated: *'Plerumque in sacro eloquio sapientes Dei consilium trahunt a sapientibus saeculi. Sic nunc . . . (PL* 113, col. 105a): In sacred eloquence the wise men of God generally take

counsel from the wise men of the world. As in this case . . .'
The eloquence of Scripture is for the wise who can interpret
the intercourse of earthly and heavenly wisdom. In his
parables Jesus seems to instruct as clearly as possible, using
as narrative everyday situations familiar to his audience and
spelling out their allegorical meaning, yet he too suggests
that they will be understood only by the enlightened: 'Qui
habet aures audiendi, audiat (Mark IV, 9): He that hath ears to
hear, let him hear'.

The Prologue to Henryson's Morall Fabillis offers two basic
justifications for allegory. The author sets them down
placidly, apparently unconcerned that they represent two
opposing views of allegory or, if not incompatible, two ends
of a spectrum of allegorical theory:

Thocht feinyeit fabils of ald poetre
Be not al grunded upon truth, yit than
Thair polite termes of sweit rhetore
Richt plesand ar unto the eir of man;
And als the caus that thay first began
Wes to repreif the haill misleving
Off man be figure of ane uther thing.


In lyke maner as throw the bustious eird,
Swa it be laubourit with grit diligence,
Springis the flouris and the corne abreird,
Hailsum and gude to mannis sustenence,
Sa dois spring ane moral sweit sentence
Oute of the subtell dyte of poetry,
To gude purpois quha culd it weill apply.


The nuttis schell, thocht it be hard and teuch,
Haldis the kirnill [sueit and delectabill;]
Sa lyis thair ane doctrine wyse aneuch
And full of frute under ane fenyeit fabill;
And clerkis sayis it is richt profitabill
Amongis ernist to ming ane merie sport,
To light the spreit and gar the tyme be schort.

Forthermair, ane bow that is ay bent
Worthis unsmart and dullis on the string;
Sa dois the mynd that is ay diligent
In ernistfull thochtis and in studying:
With sad materis sum merines to ming
Accordis weill: thus Esope said, I wis:
'Dulcius arrident seria picta Iocis.'[10]

The 'fable' is alternatively seen as a delightful surface, 'sweit', 'plesand', 'merie', light relief among serious matters, and as a strenuous challenge, demanding strength and perseverance, a 'hard and teuch' shell. In the first stanza the rhetoric is described as 'sweit', in the second and third the meaning: 'a moral sweit sentence'; 'the kirnill sueit and delectabill'. In the second stanza 'diligence' is required to work out the meaning from the fable; in the fourth the 'diligent' mind, occupied with study, should be allowed the recreation of fable. Henryson proposes two different views almost simultaneously: that the charm and entertainment of fable are necessary to lure the weak to instruction and to relax the studious; and that fable provides a hard way of making the audience work for a delightful moral, so that only the devoted will receive the instruction and will value it more for the pains they have taken.

Henryson's view that allegorical poetry is, as well as delightful recreation, a stern test, follows the tradition of medieval commentary on Scripture. In a metaphor similar to that of nut and shell, Bede describes the process of Biblical interpretation as 'a stripping off the bark of the letter to find a deeper and more sacred meaning in the pith of the spiritual sense' (Preface to the Commentary on *Ezra*). This passage concurs with Bede's treatise on the metrical art, in which he insists that an understanding of figures and tropes, among them *metaphora*, *allegoria*, *ironia* and *aenigma*, is indispensable for the elucidation of Scripture.[11] His sense of connection between poetry and Scripture, figurative language and numinous opacity, is shared by other exegetes. J. W. H. Atkins describes a similar attitude in Jerome:

In commenting on certain obscure passages of the Bible Jerome implies that such obscurity was inherent in poetry itself. The poet's (and the prophet's) business, he asserts, was not to speak plainly, but to speak in such terms as only the initiated could understand. This, he explained, would prevent the poet's truths from becoming cheap and vulgar; it would also render his truths more precious, seeing that they were won only after effort.[12]

In *Pearl in its Setting*[13] Ian Bishop discusses the ways in which allegory both conceals and reveals, the allegorical poles of *aenigma* and apocalyptic symbolism. *Aenigma* serves for concealment, apocalyptic symbolism for revelation. *Aenigma* is justified by the enigmatic character of much of the Scriptures and makes the audience work for the meaning. It acknowledges the mystery of the sacred in its sense of 'otherness'. Apocalyptic symbolism employs 'otherness' because there is no earthly language available to denote the heavenly. As far as revelation is possible, it demands metaphor. The most common source of such symbolism was the *Apocalypse* itself, 'an authoritative basis for . . representations of heaven'.[14] The *Apocalypse* was also, however, viewed by many commentators as an extended *aenigma*, itself requiring stern efforts of exegesis. The narrator of *Pearl* dreams of: literally, a small child; the *aenigma* of a pearl; the apocalyptic symbol of a visionary body. The pearl symbol is used here both as *aenigma* and as apocalyptic vision of heaven. Bishop emphasises the element of irony, of fluctuation between vehicle and tenor in medieval allegory. Irony was, indeed, considered by the rhetoricians as a branch of allegory, both ways of 'saying one thing meaning another'.[15] A suspicion that allegory is tautological is evidently at odds with the medieval view of its irony and mystery.

I want briefly to consider the allegory of *Piers Plowman* in terms of irony, *aenigma*, apocalypse and some of the relationships between these allegorical purposes. At the beginning of this chapter I stressed the connection between didactic allegory and Christian revelation. As an 'agnostic' reader I sometimes felt inclined to criticise a spurious clarity in allegorical procedures. Yet the allegory of the story of Meed works for the clarification of difficult material, attacks preconceptions and facile analogies. Its method is analytical and enquiring. But the enigmatic is as powerful a feature of

Langland's allegory. I want now to indicate how apocalypse and *aenigma*, apparently opposite extremes, shade into each other in *Piers Plowman* and in the general scheme of Christian theology.

Bishop uses several examples from *Piers Plowman*. Patience's riddle, which holds Dowel, is an *aenigma* (XIII 151–7). Human intelligence and learning are vexed by it: Clergy is contemptuous that Conscience should 'yernen to rede redels' (XIII 184).[16] But the enigmatic wisdom of Patience is endorsed by Conscience, who chooses to leave Clergy and accompany him. It is sanctioned by the earlier admission of Clergy that Piers has 'impugned' all the sciences (XIII 124–5). On the view that the pardon is an attack on indulgences and the tearing of the pardon an acceptance of its message, Bishop sees the episode as ironic, tenor and vehicle in contradiction. The allegorical meaning of the tearing of the pardon is the opposite of the literal.

Bishop does not discuss examples of apocalyptic symbolism from *Piers Plowman* but it is easy to supply them. Holy Church's description of the 'plente of pees' (I 152–158) evokes the mystery of the Incarnation as interplay between heaviness and lightness, organic and insubstantial, in a rush of medicinal, military, vegetable and geometrical images. Piers's allegorical map of the journey to Truth (V 560–629) leads to the revelation 'Thow shalt see in þiselue truþe sitte in þyn herte/In a cheyne of charite as þow a child were . . .' (V 606–7). The image reveals the constant presence of Truth in those who follow Christ's advice to be like children (*Mark* X 15). The 'cheyne of charite', derived from Boethius, functions as gentle *ironia*, not bondage but freedom, the chain of love which holds the universe not in imprisonment but in stable harmony.[17] The most potent apocalyptic symbol, at the heart of the poem, is the presentation of the Passion as a joust in Jerusalem. Will witnesses it in his profoundest vision, the second of the inner dreams. Here the fable provides the real meaning of the Crucifixion in contrast with the literal appearance. Apparently shame, defeat and death, it is truly a victorious battle against evil. And here, strangely, if we consider God's allegory of 'facts', we find a contradiction between vehicle and tenor. Christianity depends as much on profound ironies as on direct analogies: paradoxical relationships between loss and gain, triumph and defeat, life and death.

Langland shows himself aware of the rationale of *aenigma*, that wisdom should be dearly bought and is not the automatic right of the frivolous or impatient, when Study forbids Wit to instruct the Dreamer:

> [Studie] blamed hym and banned hym and bad hym be
>   stille –
> 'Wiþ swiche wise wordes to wissen any sottes!'
> And seide, *'nolite mittere,* man, margery perles
> Among hogges þat han hawes at wille.
> Thei doon but drauele þeron; draf were hem leuere
> Than al þe precious perree þat in paradis wexeþ.'
>                                             X 7–12

Although Study is probably pronouncing Will unfit for any kind of spiritual understanding, the text she alludes to – *'Nolite dare sanctum canibus, neque mittatis margaritas vestras ante porcos (Matthew* VII, 6): Give not that which is holy unto the dogs, neither cast ye your pearls before swine'* – was traditionally applied to the interpretation of Scriptural allegory. The *Glossa Ordinaria* comments:

> *Eadem dicitur sanctum et margarita, id est Evangelium et sacramenta ecclesiastica . . . Margarita quae in abscondito latet et de figuris, quasi apertis conchis, eruitur gemma est pretiosa quae non potest corrumpi.* (PL 114, Col. 108c)

The holy and the pearl mean the same, that is the Gospel and the sacraments of the Church . . . The pearl which lies hidden in concealment and is plucked from figures, as if from opened shells, is a precious jewel which cannot be corrupted.[18]

Here the pearls forbidden to swine include the precious hidden meanings in the figurative language of the Bible. As in *Pearl* itself, the image from the *Apocalypse* can be used as *aenigma* as well as revelation: the pearls that were believed to grow in Heaven are not manifested nor desirable to the earth-bound.

Later, in the conversation with Anima, the Dreamer states directly that the revealed Christ is still an *aenigma* in this life:

Clerkes kenne me þat crist is in alle places
Ac I seiȝ hym neuere sooþly but as myself in a Mirour:
*Hic in enigmate, tunc facie ad faciem.*
And so I trowe trewely, by þat men telleþ of it,
Charite is noȝt chaumpions fight ne chaffare as I trowe.

XV 161–4

The tone suggests a sad, straight look at the world, too straight to appreciate the illuminating ironies in Christian allegory. Literally, Christianity is – or should be – unsullied by the military or mercantile ambitions; yet, allegorically, the joust in Jerusalem stands for the redemption; earthly meed is a discordant echo of unmerited celestial reward. The Dreamer is right, at one level, to deny that 'fight' and 'chaffare' have part in charity, yet the poem he inhabits proposes a more complex universe in which divine purpose can shine through unpromising material. In the C revision the connection between *aenigma* and figurative language is made more explicit, when the Dreamer says pessimistically to Anima:

And þow fynde hym, bote figuratifliche, a ferly me þynkeþ;
*Hic in enigmate, tunc facie ad faciem . . .*

C XVII 294

Living in an *aenigma*, perceiving figures without comprehending their meaning, is seen as the ordinary human experience. The authors of Scripture are analogous to their creator in producing both illuminations and enigmas. The Christian allegorical poet has the responsibility to give both effects. Langland can be cheaply homiletic, incompetently opaque, but both his clarity and his obscurity are functional in the context of his thought.

# 6 Objections to Allegory: Allegory as Idealism

One of the most strange and distinctive features of *Piers Plowman* is the mingling of literal and allegorical characters. Literal characters appear in the dreams, personifications on some occasions in the waking interludes; throughout the poem beings with quite different fictional status – actual people, representative types, hypostatisations, rats and mice of fable tradition, typological figures – meet, talk, interact and inhabit the same kaleidoscopic landscape. We are first introduced in the vision of the field of folk not only to a spectrum of English fourteenth-century society but to a cast more varied in their modes of being than that of any other poem I know. On first encountering *Piers* most students comment on its unique diversity of characters and find the effect bizarre and intriguing.

Yet the function of this diversity has not been much discussed. Recent criticism of *Piers* has been particularly concerned with the nature of the allegory and the possible methods of interpreting it. It has therefore tended to overlook the literal elements in the poem or even, as in R. W. Frank's injunction to read the allegory literally,[1] to blur the distinction between the two modes. I suggest that the interplay between the modes forms the structural basis of the poem and that the contrast between the ranges of experience they can express is central to its meaning. Whether the allegory of *Piers Plowman* is single or multiple in significance, the mode itself suggests idealisation. It proposes a world of clear-cut moral distinctions; it deals in perfections of good or evil. By contrast, the literal mode in *Piers* presents a world of compromise, confusion and frequent indifference to moral issues.

The poem opens with the the usual conventions of the dream vision, encouraging us to expect a beautiful land-scape, an allegorical dream and a revelation of spiritual insight. But the dream world of the Prologue disappoints and confuses. It is at once a 'wilderness', a panorama, a view of Earth, Heaven and Hell, and a mundane street scene. It is inhabited by literal and allegorical characters and most of them seem cheerfully heedless of their uncertain position between dungeon and tower. By the end of the Prologue the Dreamer himself seems to have lost his commanding view of these eschatological realities, to be submerged in 'þe maȝe' and to lack a context in which to judge what he sees.

A full and clear context is established in Passus 1 by the allegorical figure of Holy Church, whose first speech points out that the values of most of the literal characters are inadequate:

> The mooste partie of þis peple þat passeþ on þis erþe,
> Haue þei worship in þis world þei kepe no bettre;
> Of ooþer heuene þan here holde þei no tale.
>
> I 7–9

The Dreamer himself, however, does not recognise her, and in answer to his question she tells him who she is, explains the significance of the tower and the dungeon and gives him an account of some of the main Christian doctrines and obligations. She is impatient with him for his failure to recognise her and for his profession of ignorance. From her point of view this information is self-evident, avail-able to anyone through 'kynde knowyng'. For Holy Church, the problem which is to be dramatically presented in the episode of Meed, of how to place economic transac-tions in a moral perspective, is solved by a simple appeal to Scripture (I 46–57). The word 'truth', reiterated throughout her speeches, is invested with final authority at the end of the passus when she suggests that she is leaving the

Dreamer with a framework which will provide adequate
moral guidance for him:

Forþi I seye as I seide er by siȝte of þise textes:
Whan alle tresors ben tried treuþe is þe beste.
Now haue I told þee what truþe is, þat no tresor is bettre,
I may no lenger lenge; now loke þee oure lord.

I 206–9

The Prologue and first passus present us with a sharp
contrast between literal and allegorical statements, almost
between a practical and an idealistic way of looking at the
world. At this point the reader is inclined to endorse the
allegorical mode as presenting more of truth than the literal
mode and the allegorical character of Holy Church as possessing the finest perception and the most informed judgment. Initially, we might say that the function of the
allegorical mode is to correct and literal. But in the course of
the poem allegorical characters come to be seen as variously
inadequate, and the collision of the allegorical and the literal
becomes more complex and disturbing. I can present this
interpretation most clearly by focusing on the episodes
involving Conscience, the personification of the faculty
which distinguishes between what is and what ought to be,
between the actual and the ideal, or, frequently in this poem,
between the claims of the literal and the allegorical.

The possibility that there might be limitations and falsifica-
tions in the allegorical, idealised mode of vision becomes
clear in the episode of Meed. Despite Holy Church's implication that she has left the Dreamer with all the answers, he
requests to be taught how to recognise the false. He is at
once shown Meed and the controversy about her marriage.
Various evil characters are interested in marrying Meed to
False; the King would prefer to marry Conscience, who
offers his definition of Meed (see Chapter 5, p. 100) and
refuses to accept her unless commanded by Reason. Peace
brings a plea against Wrong and Meed reveals her nature by
attempting to buy Wrong off. Reason condemns Meed and
'alle riȝtfulle' (IV 157) agree with him. Most of the court call
her a whore and there is no more talk of a marriage between
her and Conscience. The King asks Reason to stay with him

and Reason agrees, provided that Conscience will also be present. This story may seem rather inconclusive, particularly in its hasty shelving of the possibility of marriage between Meed and Conscience, and as an allegory it provides no satisfaction to the moralist other than the recognition of Meed's evil nature. It would be easy to sketch out an alternative fable in which Meed should represent Reward rather than Bribery (or, in Langland' s terms, include in her nature 'measurable hire'): she would then be morally neutral rather than permanently evil and could be reformed by being married to Conscience rather than to False. Such a story might seem at first to provide a more satisfying narrative and a more interesting moral. If, however, we regard Langland's story as deliberately frustrating the desire for allegorical tidiness, it appears more subtle and more profound. The quarrel between Wrong and Peace affords not only evidence against Meed but also proof of Langland's awareness of formal and moral problems inherent in allegorical writing. Since the nature of Peace is peaceful, peace-loving, peace-making *and nothing else*, his willing acceptance of the bribe and his readiness to forgive are inevitable. His response is perfect in one sense but foolish in another. The King points out that if Wrong is set free he will commit other crimes, and Reason refuses to have pity on Wrong until everyone in the world behaves perfectly and Meed has lost her power. In an ideal world, therefore. the ideal response of Peace would be appropriate; in the world as it is recognised to be by the King and by Reason it is a good response which will lead to further harm. Peace needs to be restrained almost as much as Wrong does. That Langland refuses to accommodate his realistic assessment of human behaviour in the simple moral scheme encouraged by the allegorical mode is further shown in the abandoning of the plan to marry Meed to Conscience. Such a union is no more than theoretically convenient: it could take place only in the ideal world sketched out by Reason in which he could have pity on Wrong. Since man is sinful his economic behaviour is corrupt; if Langland had married Meed to Conscience he would have denied this fact. The understandable desire of the King that they should be reconciled – 'Ye shul sauȝtne, forsoþe, and serue me boþe' (IV 2) – has to be frustrated by Conscience.

If Langland is suspicious of the idealising imagination as manifested in allegory, he is also deeply sympathetic towards it. Throughout the poem he pours scorn on literalism of belief. In Passus I it is condemned by Holy Church:

Chastite wiþouten charite worþ cheyned in helle;
It is as lewed as a lampe þat no liȝt is Inne.
Manye Chapeleyns arn chaste ac charite is aweye;
Are non hardere þan hij whan þei ben auaunced,
Vnkynde to hire kyn and to alle cristene,
Chewen hire charite and chiden after moore.
Swich chastite wiþouten charite worþ cheyned in helle.

I 188–94

The Samaritan also insists on the primacy of the spirit, the worthlessness of any religious observance which does not spring from charity:

Be vnkynde to þyn euenecristene and al þat þow kanst bidde,
Delen and do penaunce day and nyght euere,
And purchace al þe pardon of Pampilon and Rome,
And Indulgences ynowe, and be *ingratus* to þi kynde,
The Holy goost hereþ þee noȝt . . .'

XVII 254–8

Langland's attack on literalism is made most dramatically in the scene of the tearing of the pardon, which anticipates the Samaritan's condemnation of indulgences. The priest, the Dreamer and, I think, the reader are surprised when the pardon is produced. After about a hundred lines of detailed paraphrase of its message, the brevity of the actual document is disconcerting:

'Piers,' quod a preest þoo, 'þi pardon moste I rede,
For I shal construe ech clause and kenne it þee on englissh.'
And Piers at his preiere þe pardon vnfoldeþ,
And I bihynde hem boþe biheld al þe bulle.
In two lynes it lay and noȝt a lettre moore,
And was writen riȝt þus in witnesse of truþe:

*Et qui bona egerunt ibunt in vitam eternam;*
*Qui vero mala in ignem eternum.*

VII 107–14

The Dreamer's implied amazement at the form of the pardon is exactly paralleled in Passus XVII when Hope tells him of the covenant he made with God and of receiving the commandments:

He plukkede forþ a patente, a pece of an hard roche
Wheron was writen two wordes . . .

XVII 11–12

On these occasions the Dreamer seems to feel for a moment that 'two lines' and ' a piece of hard rock' cannot contain the vast meanings which are assigned to the pardon and the patent by Piers and Hope; initially, that is, he has difficulty in accepting the validity of a symbol.

There is another feature of contemporary religious life which Langland attacks at the literal level but approves in a symbolic sense – the pilgrimage. In the Prologue he condemns the actual instances of pilgrims and palmers in the field full of folk:

Pilgrymes and Palmeres pliȝten hem togidere
For to seken Seint Iame and Seintes at Rome;
Wenten forþ in hire wey wiþ many wise tales,
And hadden leue to lyen al hire lif after.
I seiȝ somme þat seiden þei hadde ysouȝt Seintes;
To ech a tale þat þei tolde hire tonge was tempred to lye
Moor þan to seye sooþ, it semed bi hire speche.

Prol. 46–52

And the pilgrim in Passus V, covered with souvenirs of his journeys, has never heard of Saint Truth. Immediately after the meeting with this pilgrim, Piers is introduced for the first time and recommends to the seekers an *allegorical* pilgrimage. This speech with its somewhat automatic allegorisation of Christian precepts as stages in the journey ('And so boweþ forþ by a brook, beþ-buxom-of-speche,/Forto ye fynden a ford, youre-fadres-honoureþ . . . The croft hatte

Coueite-no3t-mennes-catel-ne-hire-wyues-/Ne-noon-of-hire-seruaunt3-þat-noyen-hem-my3te' (V 566–7, 573–4)) is a passage where Langland's method could be criticised as being mechanical and lacking in vividness. I would reply that a more detailed and even in one sense more interesting allegory might well have defeated the purpose here: the pilgrimage has to be recognised simply as allegorical and therefore inward. The method declares the meaning bluntly and uncompromisingly. Literal characters, in their preference for outward and visible signs, are prone to translate spiritual commands into material terms. From time to time it is suggested that the wanderings of the Dreamer constitute a too physical search for Dowel which should be found within himself:

'Dowel', quod he, 'and dobet and dobest þe þridde
Arn þre faire vertues, and ben no3t fer to funde.'

VIII 78–9

'Sire Dowel dwelleþ', quod Wit, 'no3t a day hennes'

IX 1

The allegorical mode as used in Piers's advice to the pilgrims is designed effectively to prevent such misunderstanding.

The *Dowel* section of the poem is particularly concerned with intellectual enquiry, the relationship between theoretical understanding and moral development, and the possible Christian attitudes towards learning. During the first half of *Dowel* most of the characters whom the Dreamer meets are mental faculties or aspects of learning: Wit, Study, Clergy, Scripture, Imaginatif. In Passus XIII the more specifically moral qualities are re-introduced, Patience and Conscience, together with a literal character, the doctor of divinity, and we find again the tension between the modes of vision appropriate to literal and to allegorical characters and another dilemma in which Conscience has to choose a lesser good because total goodness is for the moment unattainable. The scene is a dinner party at which the Dreamer, Conscience, Clergy and the doctor of divinity are joined by Patience who is wearing pilgrim's clothes. The doctor of divinity

outrages the Dreamer who has heard him preach in favour of
abstinence by eating and drinking too much. The Dreamer
and the allegorical characters, on the other hand, are served
with purely spiritual food:

> Conscience curteisly þo commaunded Scripture
> Bifore Pacience breed to brynge, bitynge apart,
> And me þat was his mette oþer mete boþe.
> He sette a sour loof toforn vs and seide '*Agite penitenciam*',
> And siþþe he drouȝ vs drynke, *Diu perseuerans*,
> 'As longe', quod he, 'as lif and lycame may dure'.
> 'Here is propre seruice', quod Pacience, 'þer fareþ no
> Prince bettre.'

XIII 46–52

Will's reaction is quite different from that of Patience:

> Pacience was proud of þat propre seruice
> And made him murþe wiþ his mete, ac I morned
> euere . . .

XIII 59–60

Presumably only an allegorical character could be fully
satisfied with such a meal. The unnatural quality of his
holiness is underlined by the vocabulary: where Will
'mourns', Patience finds 'pride' in humility and 'mirth' in
deprivation. The use of allegory can seem almost comically
idealistic to the literal characters, as in the next passus when
Patience attempts to comfort Hawkin:

> 'And I shal purueie þee paast', quod Pacience, 'þouȝ no
> plouȝ erye,
> And flour to fede folk wiþ as best be for þe soule;
> Thouȝ neuere greyn growed, ne grape vpon vyne,
> All þat lyueþ and lokeþ liflode wolde I fynde
> And þat ynogh; shal noon faille of þyng þat hem nedeþ:
> *Ne soliciti sitis &c; Volucres celi deus pascit &c; pacientes*
> *vincunt &c.*'
> Thanne laughed haukyn a litel and lightly gan swerye;
> 'Whoso leueþ yow, by oure lord! I leue noȝt he be
> blessed.'

'No?' quod Pacience paciently, and out of his poke hente
Vitailles of grete vertues for alle manere beestes
And seide, 'lo! here liflode ynogh, if oure bileue be trewe.
For lent neuere was lif by liflode were shapen,
Whereof or wherfore or wherby to libbe . . .
*Non in solo pane viuit homo set in omni verbo quod procedit de
ore dei.'*
But I listnede and lokede what liflode it was
That pacience so preisede, and of his poke hente
A pece of þe Paternoster and profred vs alle;
And þanne was it *fiat voluntas tua* sholde fynde vs alle.
'Haue, haukyn', quod Pacience, 'and et þis whan þe
hungreþ
Or whan þow clomsest for cold or clyngest for drye.'

XIV 29–52

Here the purely allegorical nature of Patience seems to be
stressed in the phrase 'quod Pacience paciently' and the gulf
between him and the other characters expressed in
Haukyn's derision and the Dreamer's surprise ('*But* I listnede and lokede') when he sees what Patience is really
offering. Man does not live by bread alone, but that does not
make bread as dispensable as Patience implies. Similarly at
the dinner party the allegorical characters are completely
satisfied with their insubstantial meal whereas the Dreamer
is naturally enough angered by comparing it with that of the
doctor of divinity.

The dinner party concludes in a discussion, started by the
Dreamer, of the ·nature of Dowel. Clergy says that he is
unable to give a definition since Piers Plowman considers all
sciences valueless compared with love, and Conscience
turns to Patience:

Pacience haþ be in many place, and paraunter knoweþ
That no clerk ne kan, as crist bereþ witnesse:
*Pacientes vincunt &c.*

XIII 134–5

Patience quotes the counsel of Love, which will turn even
enemies to friends. He carries' Dowel' with him in a riddle:
anyone who takes it will be protected from every physical

adversity and all people including those in the highest positions of authority must feel bound to obey. At this point the doctor of divinity interrupts:

> 'It is but a dido', quod þis doctour, 'a disours tale.
> Al þe wit of þis world and wiȝt mennes strengþe
> Kan noȝt parfournen a pees bitwene þe pope and hise enemys,
> Ne bitwene two cristene kynges kan no wiȝt pees make
> Profitable to eiþer peple;' and putte þe table fro hym,
> And took Clergie and Conscience to conseil as it were
> That Pacience þo most passe, 'for pilgrymes konne wel lye'.

XIII 172–8

The doctor of divinity is the least sympathetic character in this scene, but if his speech is brutal it is also realistic. The literal mode is now correcting the allegorical. The doctor's first line points out that the speeches of the allegorical characters operate only at a fictional level: when we look at the actual condition of the world we are swiftly disillusioned. At the same time his blindness to spiritual realities is suggested in his dismissal of Patience as a mendacious pilgrim. Langland initially characterised pilgrims as liars in the Prologue (line 49) but an allegorical personage in pilgrim's clothes must be accepted: he is the ideal which actual pilgrims do not represent. Therefore the doctor of divinity, by failing to realise that Patience in pilgrim's clothes is in a different category from actual pilgrims, betrays himself as only literal-minded. He knows what the world is like, but he has no idea of what it ought to be.

Conscience now makes the decision to go on pilgrimage with Patience rather than learn with Clergy:

> Ac Conscience carped loude and curteisliche seide,
> 'Frendes, fareþ wel', and faire spak to clergie,
> 'For I wol go wiþ þis gome, if god wol yeue me grace,
> And be Pilgrym wiþ pacience til I haue preued moore.'
> 'What!' quod Clergie to Conscience, 'ar ye coueitous nouþe
> After yeresȝeues or ȝiftes, or yernen to rede redels?

I shal brynge yow a bible, a book of þe olde lawe,
And lere yow if yow like þe leeste point to knowe
That Pacience þe pilgrym parfitly knew neuere.'
'Nay, by crist!' quod Conscience . . .

Thus curteisliche Conscience congeyed first þe frere,
And siþen softeliche he seide in clergies ere,
'Me were leuere, by oure lord, and I lyue sholde,
Haue pacience parfitliche þan half þi pak of bokes.'
Clergie of Conscience no congie wolde take,
But seide ful sobreliche, 'þow halt se þe tyme
Whan þow art wery forwalked; wille me to counseille.'
'That is sooþ', seide Conscience, 'so me god helpe.
If Pacience be oure partyng felawe and pryue with vs boþe
Ther nys wo in þis world pat we ne sholde amende;
And conformen kynges to pees; and alle kynnes londes,
Sarsens and Surre, and so forþ alle þe Iewes,
Turne into þe trewe feiþ and intil oon bileue.'
'That is sooþ', seide Clergie, 'I se what þow menest.
I shal dwelle as I do my deuoir to shewe,
And conformen fauntekyns ooþer folk ylered
Til Pacience haue preued þee and parfit þee maked.'
Conscience þo wiþ Pacience passed, pilgrymes as it were.
                                        XIII 179–88, 199–215

For the moment, despite the vindication of learning given by
Imaginatif to the Dreamer (XII 72–191), virtue and learning
seem to be opposed. Each is presented as a perfection
incompatible with the other. Clergy claims that Patience
never 'parfitly knew' the details of learning; Conscience
retorts that he would rather 'haue pacience parfitliche þan
half þi pak of bokes!' Conscience feels that he must at
present choose between Clergy and Patience: union with
both of them would be ideal but is not possible. Such a union
could put right all the ills of the world, but, as in the story of
Meed, the happy ending is proposed only at the level of
prophecy. It could change the imperfect world that the
doctor reminded them of, but it cannot do it yet. Conscience's choice here is analogous to his rejection of Meed,
but the reasons for it are less obvious. He is not, after all,
rejecting an evil character but a character with great poten-

tiality for good. His decision is received 'ful sobreliche' by Clergy who says that he will return. He and Clergy begin replies to each other with the phrase 'that is sooþ', suggesting a good deal of mutual understanding and agreement. The withdrawal of Conscience is most intelligible if seen as a response to the relationship between the literal and allegorical characters of the doctor of divinity and Clergy. Clergy himself may be suspect if an actual cleric can be so blind to idealism. To exemplify Patience, even imperfectly, must be virtuous; to exemplify Clergy imperfectly need not be. When learning and virtue perfectly unite, this distinction will be invalid; at the moment both the truth and the cynicism of the doctor's speech show that this is not the case. To accept the present situation would be either cynically pragmatic or naïvely idealistic. Therefore Conscience chooses to go on pilgrimage, to suffer with Patience until he has been made fit to return to Clergy. Clergy finally endorses this decision: he must continue to perform the actions characteristic of his nature, but he agrees that the first steps towards perfection have to be taken with Patience rather than with himself.

Finally, I shall consider the behaviour of Conscience during the last part of the poem, *Dobest*. These two passus are concerned with the story of mankind after the Resurrection and with the struggle of the Church against the forces of evil. After the apparently final triumph of Christ in *Dobet*, Langland is working back to the situation with which the poem opened, the field full of folk, but its worldliness is now more sinister because seen with greater understanding. The drift towards pessimism in the last part of the poem is mainly expressed through the decline in the position of Conscience. At the beginning of Passus XIX the importance of his role as man's distinguishing faculty is emphasised: in a long passage (XIX 12–198) he explains the symbolic function of Piers Plowman and relates the stages of the ministry of Christ to the terms Dowel, Dobet and Dobest. He announces the gift of grace to the Church (XIX 207–9) and is regarded by Grace as the supreme authority within man: ' . . . crouneþ Conscience kyng' (XIX 256). Enormous reliance is placed on Conscience and, even in Passus XX when Anti-Christ is assailing the church, we are told that he alone is indestructible: 'Kynde . . . shal come at þe laste/And kille al erþely creature saue conscience oone.' (XX 150–1).

But during these last two passus the position of Conscience becomes increasingly vulnerable. As the keeper of Unity, the Church, he faces not only direct attack but, more insidiously, the perversion of values until he, of all faculties, will not be able to distinguish between right and wrong:

> Thise two [Surquidous and Spille-loue, sent by Pride]
>    coome to Conscience and to cristen peple
> And tolde hem tidynges, þat tyne þei sholde
> The sedes þat sire Piers sew, þe Cardynale vertues.
> 'And Piers bern worþ ybroke; and þei þat ben in vnitee
> Shulle come out, Conscience; and youre caples two,
> Confession and Contricion, and your carte þe bileeue
> Shall be coloured so queyntely and couered vnder oure
>    Sophistrie
> That Conscience shal noȝt knowe who is cristene or
>    heþene,
> Ne no manere marchaunt þat wiþ moneye deleþ
> Wheiþer he wynne wiþ right, wiþ wrong or wiþ vsure.'
>
> XIX 341–50

We see their prediction fulfilled immediately in the perversion of the cardinal virtues when the lord describes how his auditor, steward and clerks deal with his reeve's accounts:

> Wiþ *Spiritus Intellectus* þei toke þe reues rolles
> And wiþ *Spiritus fortitudinis* fecche it, wole he, nel he
>
> XIX 463–4

and the more problematic cases of the king who claims that he can take anything from his country 'of *Spiritus Iusticie*' (XIX 474) and the poor man who, according to Need, is free to beg and steal 'by techynge and by tellynge of *spiritus temperancie*' (XX 8).

In the presentation of this dilemma the 'lewd vicar' seems to play a similar role to that of the doctor of divinity. When Conscience exclaims to the brewer who will not deal according to Justice, the voice of a literal character interrupts:

'But Conscience be þi comunes and Cardinale vertues
Leue it wel þow art lost, boþe lif and soule'.
'Thanne is many a lif lost', quod a lewed vicory.
'I am a Curatour of holy kirke, and cam neuere in my tyme
Man to me þat me kouþe telle of Cardinale vertues,
Or þat acountede Conscience at a cokkes feþere.
I knew neuere Cardynal þat he ne cam fro þe pope.
And we clerkes, whan þei come, for hir comunes paieþ'
                                                XIX 407–14

The vicar thinks as concretely as the doctor of divinity who
misjudges Patience in his pilgrim's clothes: he cannot attach
the word 'cardinal' to anything but actual people, but, and
partly *for* this reason, his judgment of the cardinals is
realistic. He ends his speech with an exact analysis of the
perversion of intellect present in *Dobest*:

For *Spiritus prudencie* among þe peple is gyle,
And alle þo faire vertues as vices þei semeþ.
Ech man subtileþ a slei3te synne to hide
And coloureþ it for a konnynge and a clene lyuynge.
                                                XIX 455–8

The Vicar may only see the actual, but he sees that more
clearly than some of the allegorical characters do.

These themes – the inability of a good allegorical character
to act with full command of the situation, particularly in the
context of intellectual perversion and economic corruption,
the failure of learning to aid Conscience in the present state
of the world, and the necessity for Conscience to withdraw,
suspending immediate hope of a perfect solution – are all
brought together in the closing episode of the poem.

Unity is now not only assailed from without but also
vulnerable within, and Conscience cries for help from the
perfect idea of the clergy against the actual examples of the
clergy within the church:

Conscience cryede, 'help, Clergie or I falle
Thoru3 inparfite preestes and prelates of holy chirche.'
                                                XX 228–9

The friars come to help and although Need warns Conscience that they are motivated by avarice, Conscience wel-
comes them on condition that they live according to their
rule, leave logic and learn to love. Envy immediately sends
the friars to school to learn logic and law and prove that all
things ought to be held in common. The desperate optimism
which is displayed and refuted in this episode is to character-
ise the behaviour of Conscience until the closing lines of the
poem.

Conscience makes Peace the porter of Unity. Unity is
assailed by Hypocrisy who 'woundede wel wikkedly many a
wys techere/ That wiþ Conscience acordede and Cardynale
vertues.' (XX 302–3). Conscience calls for an effective doctor
for their sickness, Shrift, who behaves appropriately: 'Shrift
shoop sharp salue and made men do penaunce' (XX 306) and
is therefore unpopular with some of the occupants of Unity
who ask for a gentler doctor such as Friar Flatterer. Surpris-
ingly, yet, in terms of the allegorical pattern which Langland
has established, inevitably, three of the virtues, Conscience,
Contrition and Peace, agree to admit him. Contrition advises
Conscience to do so 'For here is many a man hurt þoruȝ
ypocrisye.' (XX 317). Presumably he must feel that any kind
of contrition is better than none, and is therefore apt to
mistake the form of penance for the reality. Conscience
replies that they have no need of the friar and should prefer
certain authorised clergy, such as the parish priest, but then
gives in:

'I may wel suffre', seide Conscience, 'syn ye desiren,
That frere flaterere be fet and phisike yow sike.'

XX 322–3

If 'syn ye desiren' is spoken to the people within Unity in
general, it suggests that Conscience, like Contrition, has to
approve their expressed desire for penance, even if it takes
too mild a form. If, as I suppose, the phrase is addressed to
Contrition, its implications are more complex. Conscience,
whose nature is to distinguish between virtuous and vicious
action, cannot refuse the promptings of a good quality even
if this quality should be, through the limitations of its own
virtue, mistaken.

When the friar arrives at the gate and is questioned by Peace, we find that the behaviour of Peace is consistent with his forgiveness of Wrong, in the *Visio*. His choice is similarly, although it is no longer totally, blind. He tells the friar to leave and recalls the evil behaviour of one of his order, but, like Conscience, he soon capitulates:

Hende speche heet pees, 'opene þe yates.
Lat in þe frere and his felawe, and make hem fair cheere.
He may se and here here, so may bifalle,
That lif þoruȝ his loore shal leue coueitise
And be adrad of deeþ and wiþdrawe hym fram pryde
And acorde wiþ Conscience and kisse hir eiþer ooþer.'

XX 348–53

It is not made clear whose courteous speech is thus alleg-orised: if it is that of Peace, we are being shown that his nature must include courtesy even when it is inappropriate to the situation, and that he has to give the benefit of the doubt to the friar who may, despite his probable evil life, do good through his learning; the meaning is not very different if we assign the courteous speech to the friar, but Peace's reaction to it is then even more clearly parallel to his behaviour in the episode with Wrong. He has to react favourably to any friendly overture, no matter how decep-tive it may be.

The friar's first patient is Contrition himself whose illness has been mentioned by Peace. At this point again I think that the allegorical mode demands attention in itself as well as simple translation into literal terms. Of course the literal sense of Contrition's illness is that most of the Christians within the Church are rarely or never contrite. But in this context to say that 'Contrition is sick' seems to demand scrutiny of virtue itself as well as condemnation of those who fail to achieve it. Whitaker commented upon Conscience's reception of the friar as a possible doctor for Contrition: 'There is an impropriety in this; it was not the part of Conscience to complain that the parish priest was too severe a confessor.'[2] Where Langland commits apparent allegorical improprieties, I think that the breakdown of pure allegory is purposeful: an attack is made on the habit of thought it encourages. The illness of Contrition is, after all, almost as 'out of character' as the speech of Conscience which it provokes. If a virtue becomes impossible for anybody to practise effectively, the concept of the virtue itself must be weakened. The feeble state of Contrition explains the 'improper' reaction of Conscience. Conscience, no longer advised by Reason as he was in the *Visio*, is in the state of moral and intellectual confusion which is one of the themes of *Dobest*. The failure of a virtue is so shocking that the allegorical mode itself is temporarily endangered: Conscience begins to compromise and suggest half-measures as though he were a literal rather than an allegorical example of Conscience.

If in this passage Langland has been suggesting criticisms and attempting violations of the allegorical method, he goes on to achieve his most destructive effect in the next lines where he describes Contrition's reaction to the comfort of the friar:

> Til Contricion hadde clene foryeten to crye and to wepe
> And wake for hise wikked werkes as he was wont to
> doone.
> For confort of his confessour Contricion he lafte,
> XX 369–71

The irony of the last line quoted hammers home the reversal of values which Conscience is confronting. If Contrition can be thus denatured, Conscience can no longer rely on any of the traditional moral categories, and after a final unanswered cry for help he sets out again on a pilgrimage:

> Conscience cryed eft Clergie to helpe,
> And bad Contricion come to kepe þe yate.
> 'He lyþ adreynt and dremeþ,' seide Pees, 'and so do
> manye oþere.
> The frere wiþ his phisyk þis folk haþ enchaunted,
> And doþ men drynke dwale; þei drede no synne.'
> 'By crist!' quod Conscience þo, 'I wole bicome a pilgrym,
> And wenden as wide as þe world renneþ
> To seken Piers þe Plowman, þat pryde my3te destruye,
> And þat freres hadde a fyndyng þat for nede flateren

And countrepledeþ me, Conscience; now kynde me
   avenge,
And send me hap and heele til I haue Piers þe Plowman.'
And siþþe he gradde after Grace til I gan awake.

XX 375–86

Conscience has in earlier episodes in the poem been a
partially isolated figure, obliged because of the imperfection
of the world to make choices which seemed inconvenient or
even perverse to other virtuous characters. But when he
refused the king's suggestion that he should marry Meed he
was supported by Reason and when he left Clergy he was
accompanied by Patience. Now in the total corruption of the
world as represented by the metamorphosis of Contrition
he is totally alone. His cry to Clergy presumably expresses a
need for intellectual and moral guidance but there is no reply
to it. It echoes the earlier appeal – 'help, Clergie or I
falle/Thoruȝ inparfite preestes' (XX 228–9) – to an idea of
perfection which is breaking down. After the dinner Clergy
predicted that conscience would finally need his counsel and
refused to say goodbye to him (XIII 202–4), but now he fails
to appear. The gap between the ideal and the actual which
Conscience perceived in the earlier episode has widened
disastrously. Even the awareness of the narrator which has
been developing throughout the poem is casually discredited in Peace's 'He [Contrition] lyþ . . . and dremeþ . . . and
so do manye oþere.' After so many assumptions have been
destroyed, the poem ends, as it began, with the search for
Truth. But the Church is no longer a perfect mentor who can
provide the truth. It is Unity whose name points to an ideal
which its nature belies. Having first rejected in Meed an evil
quality, then in Clergy a capacity which can be used for good
or ill, Conscience finally withdraws from the guardian of
virtues because in an imperfect world virtue may take less
than perfect forms. Yet the allegorical mode, almost destroyed by the co-existence of the literal, is finally asserted in
the recourse of Conscience to the symbol of the pilgrim.

   This analysis assumes that Langland was self-conscious in
his opposition of the allegorical and literal modes and seeks
to demonstrate that he questioned the habits of thought
inherent in allegory. It therefore depends on a very different

view of allegory from that presented by C. S. Lewis. In *The Allegory of Love* Lewis quotes Dante's remark that 'love has not, like a substance, an existence of its own, but is only an accident occurring in a substance' and states: 'Symbolism is a mode of thought, but allegory is a mode of expression. It belongs to the form of poetry more than to its content.'[3] My view that the limitations of Peace are exposed in the Meed episode could be criticised on the ground that Peace is not in fact a 'substance' but an 'accident occurring in a substance': in an actual personality Peace would operate in conjunction with other qualities such as Reason and be tempered by them. There are several possible replies to this objection. One could, for example, argue from the form of the poem that, since Peace is presented by Langland as a distinct character, the reader does not naturally place him in a synthesis which is unattempted by the author. Or one could make an appeal to 'real life' and observe that such qualities as peacefulness and patience, however virtuous, are not necessarily the most effective in dealing with morally complex situations. Neither of these arguments seems to me totally satisfactory: the first is too allegorical, the second too literal. It seems preferable in discussing this poem to assert that allegory is a mode of thought which Langland is investigating and defining through the juxtaposition of allegorical and literal. This reading suggests that the allegorical habit of thought is indispensable in formulating moral concepts, but that, since these concepts are modified by actual situations, allegorisation itself comes under increasing suspicion. By the end of the poem the mode has been so strained that 'perfect' characters behave inconsistently. Yet the desire for the idealism and intellectual coherence of allegory cannot be abandoned. The final image of the pilgrim reinstates the allegorical, not as a statement of a scheme, but in terms of a quest for the unknown.

# 7 A Note on Miracles

'For I pray God to bless improvements in gardening till London be a city of palm trees,' wrote Christopher Smart.[1] The peculiar charm of this petition lies less in the unlikeliness of London miraculously transfigured into the New Jerusalem than in its deranged practicality. It is much easier to imagine London instantly transformed by divine fiat than by a long process of improbable technical developments. The symbol of Jerusalem as Christian soul and heavenly City is traditional and satisfying: Chaucer can allude easily to the New Jerusalem, figured by Canterbury, as the true destination of pilgrimage; Vaughan can evoke the lost purity of childhood in the image of 'that shady city of palm trees'.[2] Neither poet is demanding the same act of faith as Smart; neither provokes such amused, if affectionate, scepticism. Smart takes a conventional allegory and expands it with a devout literalism which strains credulity.

In poetry, miracle and allegory are close relations. We may say that miracle transforms the allegorical into the literal, reifies its meaning a stage further. But there are imaginative dangers in this procedure. Smart treats it with an extreme of literalness which argues absolute belief and partial insanity. It would be easier to assent to a leap of faith than to his series of steps. It seems more decorous, if less daring, to present miracles as largely symbolic events and not invite practical scrutiny. Smart's piety is unintentionally comic, exciting – however unfairly – a response like that to the phoney modern miracle in John Mortimer's play, *Hell*, which, at a

130

moment of domestic crisis in the vicarage, provides loaves, fishes and frozen chips.

In *Piers Plowman* miracles are described both as literal facts and as symbolic messages. Langland writes of miracles several times in the *Vita*. He shows little interest in the miraculous in the *Visio* until the end, when Piers is inspired to answer the priest. The development of thought during the two sections of the poem makes the appearance of miracles more appropriate in the latter. The *Visio* is largely concerned with the approach to the practical duties of life: the first vision considers the correct attitude towards money; the second stresses the importance of honest industrious work in each vocation. Appeal to miraculous solutions would be obviously out of place here, holding out false hope to the idle and compromising the logic and realism of the argument. But when Piers announces, after the tearing of the pardon, that he will cease from sowing, work less hard, stop being 'busy' about his livelihood and turn to prayer and penance, he signals a change in the direction of the poem. The text he quotes, '*Ne solliciti sitis* (VII 131): Put away anxious thoughts' (N.E.B.),[3] might serve as epigraph for much of the *Vita*. The *Visio* emphasises the value of responsibility for one's own needs and those of society; the *Vita* the virtue of contemplation, patient poverty and trust in providence. Hawkin's pride, as 'active life', in his provision of bread for society would seem less reprehensible in the *Visio* than it does to Conscience and Patience in the *Vita*. Toiling and spinning are sternly advocated in the *Visio*. But Piers anticipates the attitude recommended in the *Vita* when, turning to his new way of life, he says that we should learn from the 'ensample' of the birds in the field that God will provide (VII 129–132). '*Fuerunt michi lacrime mee panes die ac nocte*' he quotes (VII 128): tears will serve for bread, just as in Passus XIII quotations from the Bible comprise the dinner offered to Patience and the Dreamer.

Donaldson suggests that *Visio* and *Vita* may be seen as studies in the two counsels offered by Christ to the rich young man who asked what he should do to be saved.[4] Jesus first replies with familiar instruction, a list of the commandments. He reminds his questioner of the obvious moral obligations, as Holy Church recalls to Will what both 'cristen and vncristen cleymeþ' (I 93). But neither *Piers* nor the rich young man of the story stops there. The young man says that he has observed all the commandments from his childhood: what more should he do? Jesus answers: '*Si vis perfectus esse, vade, vende quae habes et da pauperibus, et veni, sequere me*: If thou wilt be perfect, go and sell that thou hast, and give to the poor, and come, follow me.' If the young man wishes to be perfect, he must sell all he has, give the proceeds to the poor, and follow Christ; but, on hearing this, he goes away sadly. Similarly, the values recommended in the *Visio* are sufficient for salvation; the austere ideals of the *Vita* are necessary for perfection.

Because he has great possessions, the young man in the Gospel is sad at learning what Christian perfection entails. Yet there is no suggestion that the life he already leads is bad. One should accept the ethic of both *Visio* and *Vita*, even if one cannot fulfil the most extreme demands of the latter. But it is difficult not to feel that the best is the enemy of the good. In the double structure of the last passus of the *Visio* Piers's renunciation of his former virtuous life is as ambiguous as his tearing of the pardon. We respond to it as both affirmative – he proceeds from one good state to another or, perhaps, from doing well to doing better – and destructive. In the C version this speech, together with the tearing of the pardon, is omitted. Presumably Langland came to think it potentially misleading. Since many people cannot follow the path of perfection of the *Vita*, the imperatives of the *Visio* should not be disowned. Yet, just as the scene is more powerful with the tearing of the pardon, it is more intelligible with the speech which follows it. Donaldson points out that with the removal of the speech a 'vital signpost that directs the reader on the safe way to the *Vita* . . . our only indication that from this point on the poem will concern less and less the active life of society and more and more the contemplative life of the individual'[5] has been taken down.

Donaldson argues that an insertion earlier in C provides a new signpost.[6] When Piers gives his directions to the Castle of Truth, the cutpurse and apeward who retort that they have no kin there are joined by several other characters:

'ȝe, *villam emi*,' quaþ on' and now most ich þudere,

To loke how me lykeþ hit' and tok hus leue at peers.
Anoþer anon ryght nede seyde he hadde
To folwen fif ʒokes 'for-thy me by-houeþ
To gon with a good wil and greiþliche hem dryue;
For-þy ich praye ʒow, peers, paraunter, yf ʒe meteþ
Treuthe, telleþ to hym þat ich be excused.'
Thenne was þer on heihte actif, an hosebounde he semed;
'Ich haue ywedded a wyfe,' quaþ he, 'wel wantowen of
   maners;
Were ich seuenyght fro hure syghte synnen hue wolde,
And loure on me and lyghtliche chide and seye ich loue
   anoþere.
For-þy, peers plouhman, ich praye þe telle hit treuthe,
Ich may nat come for a kytte so hue cleueþ on me;
*Vxorem duxi, et ideo non possum uenire.'*
Quaþ contemplacion, 'by crist thauh ich care suffre,
Famyn and defaute folwen ich wolle peers . . .'

C VIII 292–306

Allegorically, these responses allude to the parable in *Luke*
XVI of those who refuse to come to the lord's supper;
structurally, they predict the change of emphasis from active
life in the *Visio* to contemplative life in the *Vita* and anticipate
the condemnation of active life in the person of Hawkin. But,
read literally, some of the excuses are not, in the context of
the *Visio*, sinfully perverse. The man who leaves to drive his
yokes of oxen is behaving as Piers himself will when he
insists that the ploughing of the half-acre must be performed
before the pilgrimage. The married man with the wanton
wife is showing responsibility for her soul as well as desire
for her body: the *Glossa Ordinaris*, commenting on the text '*In
eadem vocacione qua vocati estis, state* (I *Corinthians* VII 20): Let
every man abide in the same calling wherein he was called',
insists that conversion does not entail abandoning a state or
an occupation unless it is sinful, and takes marriage as its
example of a condition in which one should remain.[7] And
the narrative contradicts itself in the implication that these
speakers, with their worldly concerns, cannot approach the
Castle of Truth: Piers has already given them the same
directions to the Castle as Jesus gave the rich young man to
eternal life, the commandments.

*Piers Plowman* is formally divided into the double structure of *Visio* and *Vita*. Perhaps the organisation has an element of ironic structure. The *Vita* is both a progression from the *Visio* and a partial contradiction of it. It questions the value of worldly responsibility which the *Visio* promotes. Langland is fully aware of the problems involved in assenting to both ethics. His omission of Piers's transitional speech in C softens the fact that the ideal character makes a choice between them. Instead, his functions are distributed, in the earlier insertion, between the allegorical polarities 'actif' and 'contemplacion'.

But if C deletes some of the moral ambiguities of carelessness for the morrow in Piers, it re-introduces them in Recklessness. This character first appears in B, in ragged clothes, to encourage the Dreamer to enjoy himself, follow Fortune and not worry about the future (XI 34–36). Old age is far off and there is plenty of time for worldliness – opposite advice to the sober counsel of Imaginatif in the next passus (XII 3–10) that he should repent while he can, before infirmity makes prayer and penance even more difficult. Recklessness is an aspect of the Dreamer's angry state of mind after he concludes that there is no way in which he can ensure or improve his chance of salvation. In C he offers the same feckless advice (C XII 194–5) and in C he is assigned a version of the predestinarian speech which Will delivered in X and which was his final defiance in A (A XI 258–313, X 377–481, C XII 200–309). In B and so far in C Recklessness appears to be a figure of temptation. But in C he is double-edged: his 'carelessness' is revealed as a quality with a virtuous positive side when he goes on to recommend, at earnest length, the value of patient poverty (C XIII 99 – XIV 111) for clergy and laity. In the course of this he recounts and quotes from the counsel of perfection given by Christ to the rich young man (C XIII 160–66). In C Recklessness is described as kin to 'wanhope', despair (C XII 198), but he proves also to be a close relation of faith.[8]

Both B and C *Vitae* extol and question the virtue of poverty and lack of care for the morrow. Recklessness, as he develops in C, is an ambiguous character. Need, as he appears to the destitute Dreamer at the beginning of Passus XX, is another. Need argues that, in circumstances of extreme deprivation, one is entitled to take the basic necessities of food, drink and clothing. Will should not be ashamed to beg and be needy since Christ, who created everything, chose a life of poverty (XX 6–50). Need's account of the suffering of Christ is movingly expressed but his argument is not decisive. The meaning of the poverty of Christ had been much debated and the orthodox view was that it did not set a general example to all men to renounce all possessions. The argument raged in particular over the ideal of poverty professed by the fraternal orders.[9] Langland is strongly opposed to the friars' profession of poverty and the justification for begging based upon it. He does not believe that the friars take no thought for the morrow and he does not advise them to. On the contrary, in the last lines of the poem, Conscience, near despair at the harm done to Unity by an insinuating friar, exclaims that they should have a 'fyndyng', regular provision, rather than flatter for 'nede' (XX 383).

Despite its lauding of patient poverty, even the *Vita* is not a totally hospitable context for suggestions that God will always provide and that spiritual food is the only necessity. We have already seen how derisively Hawkin, the waferer, reacts to Patience's offer of allegorical food. At the beginning of her conversation with the Dreamer in Passus I, Holy Church stated that there were three necessities, food, drink and clothing, which God in his courtesy had ordained that the earth should yield for men (I 17–25). But Patience insists to Hawkin that the prayer '*Fiat voluntas tua*: Thy will be done' is an adequate substitute: 'et þis whan þe hungreþ/Or whan þow clomsest for cold or clyngest for drye' (XIV 51–2). Patience then shifts ground slightly to claim that, although his counsel is probably fatal, death is desirable for the good Christian: 'but deye as god likeþ/Or þoruȝ hunger or þoruȝ hete, at his wille be it;/For if þow lyue after his loore, þe shorter lif þe bettre' (XIV 58–60). As if to extricate himself from this gloss on '*Non in solo pane vivit homo, sed in omni verbo quod procedit de ore dei*: Man shall not live by bread alone but by every word that proceedeth out of the mouth of God'. Patience produces stories of God miraculously providing food and drink:

It is founden þat fourty wynter folk lyuede withouten
   tulying,
And out of þe flynt sprong þe flood þat folk and beestes
   dronken.
And in Elyes tyme heuene was yclosed
That no reyn ne roon; þus rede men in bokes,
That manye wyntres men lyueden and no mete ne
   tulieden.
Seuene slepe, as seiþ þe book, seuene hundred wynter
And lyueden wiþouten liflode and at þe laste þei
   woken . . .

                                             XIV 64–70

Patience then moves on, rather inconsequentially, to
recommend a practical application of the *mesure* principle as
a way of redistributing wealth or resources and thus prevent-
ing starvation:

And if men lyuede as mesure wolde sholde neuere moore
   be defaute
Amonges cristene creatures, if cristes wordes ben trewe.
Ac vnkyndenesse *caristiam* makeþ amonges cristen peple,
Oþer plentee makeþ pryde amonges poore and riche.
Ac mesure is so muche worþ it may noȝt be to deere . . .

                                             XIV 71–5

This analysis seems at odds with the statements of faith
Patience has already made in this speech. Here he advocates
just conduct rather than patient endurance and suggests
how human suffering might be prevented. This speech with
all its contradictions and changes of direction, its impossible
recommendations to live (or die) on the word of God, its
appeals to exemplary stories of miraculous feeding, its
inconsistent advocacy of social reform by *mesure*, may well
seem on first reading a headlong rush of improving senti-
ments in arbitrary succession. Yet it does have a tripartite
structure with its own logic: it first recommends, in its claims
for allegorical food, a position of 'reckless' detachment from
the world; it finally preaches a responsible and practical
approach to suffering and injustice; between the two are the
stories of miracles, *exempla* of both spiritual trust and divine

care for physical needs.

The idea of the miraculous seems to play a similar role in Anima's long speech to the Dreamer on the nature of Charity (XV 165–613). One of Charity's attributes is that 'The mooste liflode he lyueþ by is loue in goddes passion' (XV 255). Anima goes on to recommend that the suffering of Christ be imitated and to quote the phrase already used by Patience, 'patientes vincunt: The patient conquer' (XV 259–68). As if Langland felt these claims to be too extreme, Anima then turns, like Patience, to examples of miraculous feeding, to legends of saints who were nourished in the wilderness by animals and birds (XV 269–304). From these, Anima moves on to consider the stories as allegories and, like Patience, makes a practical recommendation about the economic ordering of society; just as the bird fed the saints, the laity should provide for the religious so that (not unexpectedly) the friars could stop begging:

Ac god sente hem foode by foweles and by no fierse
    beestes
In menynge þat meke þyng mylde þyng sholde fede.
Riȝt so Religiouses rightfulle men sholde fynde,
And lawefulle men to lifholy men liflode brynge;
And þanne wolde lordes and ladies be looþ to agulte,
And to taken of hir tenauntȝ moore þan trouþe wolde,
Founde þei þat freres wolde forsake hir almesses
And bidden hem bere it þere it yborwed was.
For we by goddes behestes abiden alwey
Til briddes brynge vs wherby we sholde lyue.

XV 305–14

Bloomfield comments on this speech: 'Anima tries to reconcile two arguments here – that God will take care of those who throw themselves "recklessly" on His Providence and that God helps those who help themselves.'[10] Patience's reference to miracles looks like a bridge between a position of world-denying austerity and a practical application of the *mesure* principle. Anima's speech also seems to modulate through the idea of the miraculous from a very spiritual to a very social position.

Anima uses the miracles of feeding as evidence that the

promises of faith will be literally made good. But he equally regards miracles as *exempla* which demand allegorical interpretation. The stories of saints fed by birds instruct us that the mild should provide for the meek and the virtuous laity support the religious. Even a spurious miracle can act as obverse of this *exemplum* and yield a moral. The legend that Mahomet trained a white dove to come, like a parody of the Holy Spirit, and appear to speak to him (XV 397–411) has allegorical relevance in Christian society: 'I dar noȝt telle truþe,/How englisshe clerkes a coluere fede þat coueitise hiȝte,/And ben manered after Makometh . . .' (XV 414–16). When Anima recalls the miracles of Christ, he treats them too primarily as *exempla*, stressing their allegorical value rather than their literal benefits:

> Whan þe hye kyng of heuene sente his sone to erþe
> Many myracles he wrouȝte men for to turne,
> In ensaumple þat men sholde se by sadde reson
> Men myȝte noȝt be saued by þoruȝ mercy and grace,
> And þoruȝ penaunce and passion and parfit bileue.
>
> XV 511–15

Anima, with his variety of names (XV 23–39), seems to be a synthesis of several of the allegorical characters we have already met in the *Vita*. His speech is an attempt to bring different values, modes of discourse and ways of knowing into harmony with each other. As Bloomfield points out, he advocates both self-help and trust in Providence. He stresses that the duty of the bishop is to provide both 'Bodily foode and goostly foode' (XV 576). He uses miracles as a way of mediating between the allegorical and the literal and respecting the claims of both. He also sees in miracles a resolution of one of Langland's favourite dichotomies, works and words, and the problem of the lack of necessary connection between them:[11] in the conversion of England, St. Augustine 'þe feiþ tauȝte/Moore þoruȝ miracles þan þoruȝ muche prechyng;/As wel þoruȝ hise werkes as wiþ hise holy wordes' (XV 448–50).

Anima interprets the miracles of Christ as *exempla*. Elsewhere in the poem Langland integrates them into the allegorical scheme of *Piers Plowman*, drawing from them a pattern of spiritual meanings more than evoking wonder at their literal occurrence. In the vision of the life of Christ in Passus XVI, there is the account of how Piers Plowman taught him lechecraft' (XVI 104), which I discussed briefly in Chapter 4. The miracles of healing are described as part of this process of learning (XVI 106–19). They act as part of the complex and delicate definition of the relationship between the perfect allegorical humanity of Piers and the perfect literal humanity and divinity of Jesus. They are practice for Christ: Piers teaches him to 'assaie his surgenrie on hem þat sike were/Til he was parfit praktisour' (XVI 106–16). Although they provide evidence for faith (XVI 117–126), the poem states that Christ did not see them as demostrations of his power: 'he held it for no maistrie' (XVI 112). *Piers* invites us to see the miracles of healing primarily as symbols by which the 'leche of lif' (XVI 118) anticipates the final victory of Life against Death.

In Passus XIX when Conscience narrates the life of Christ to Will and interprets his various names and titles, he fits the miracles into the allegorical structure of *Piers Plowman*. When Christ turned the water into wine at the marriage at Cana, 'þere bigan god of his grace to do wel' (XIX 110). When he cured the lame and the blind and fed the multitude with five loaves and two fishes, 'he confortede carefulle and caughte a gretter name/The which was dobet,' (XIX 128–9). He appeared to convince doubting Thomas of the Resurrection 'And whan þis dede was doon do best he þouʒte' (XIX 182). The life of Christ contains in symbol the three stages of human history which are one of the organising structures of the poem. The transformation of the water to wine is a figure of the fulfilling of the law of the Old Testament by the New Covenant of love. Like the end of the *Visio* it allegorises the transition from obedience to the commandments to the counsel of perfection. The miracles of healing and feeding cause him to be acknowledged by the faithful as king and lead up to the major victories described in the vision of *Dobet*, the Passion and Resurrection. After he manifests himself to Thomas, he entrusts his power to Piers, at Pentecost '*Spiritus paraclitus* ouerspradde hem alle' (XIX 206), and *Dobest* narrates the subsequent history of the Church.

There is some affront to faith in the idea of selective proof being vouchsafed to a few fortunate sceptics through miracle.

Christ himself acknowledges this when he qualifies his revelation to Thomas with '*Beati qui non viderunt et crediderunt* (*John* XX|29): Blessed are those who have not seen and yet have believed,' a statement which *Piers* quotes in conclusion of the story (XIX 181). There is also an imaginative difficulty in visualising the symbolic so literally. Langland, who has doubts about idealistic allegorical solutions to literal problems, treats miracles as a bridge between the modes. They discourage worldliness by providing literal endorsement that the divine intervenes in the field of human life. They encourage the spirit by demanding to be read as allegories.

# 8 Objections to Allegory: Allegory as Spiritualism

One traditional purpose of allegorical interpretation has been to gloss over uncomfortable literal meanings. It has been used to disinfect and elevate material which, while revered as Scripture or poetry, could at the literal level be considered immoral in tendency. In antiquity allegorical interpretations of the pantheon provided a defence against the strictures of philosophers who argued that we should not postulate of the gods attributes and actions we should think evil in men.[1] Classical culture, though pagan, was similarly preserved for the education of Christians: if Hercules could be seen as a type of Christ and Virgil's fourth eclogue as an account of the Incarnation, Latin poetry could be regarded as edifying and, in a spiritual sense, truthful.[2] Even parts of the Old Testament felt to be inconsistent with Christian precepts were purified by the concentration on allegorical meanings more uplifting than the literal sense. For example, the standard interpretation of the *Song of Songs* was that it celebrated not human love and sexuality but the love of Christ for his Church.[3] The cynicism of the Preacher's remark in *Ecclesiastes* IX, 4, that a living dog is better than a dead lion, is transformed by the *Glossa Ordinaria* into a statement of faith: '*Canis vivus, pauper iustus, leo mortuus, potens iniquus, qui nihil secum aufert de mundo* (PL 113 Col. 1124d): The living dog is the just poor man, the dead lion the wicked powerful man who takes nothing with him from the world.'

141

There have always been critical objections to this method of purifying suspect material. One of the earliest is Plato's assertion that, imaginatively, it does not really work:

> Stories like those of Hera being bound by her son, or of Hephaestus flung from heaven by his father for taking his mother's part when she was beaten, and all those battles of the gods in Homer, must not be admitted into our state, whether they be allegorical or not. A child cannot distinguish the allegorical sense from the literal, and the ideas he takes in at that age are likely to become indelibly fixed.[4]
>
> *Republic* II, 378

In his second Prologue to the *Glossa Ordinaria* Nicholas de Lyra insists that the literal sense of Scripture must be primarily respected and that an allegorical interpretation in conflict with it should be thought improper:

> Omnes [expositiones mysticae] tamen praesupponunt sensum literalem tanquam fundamentum. Unde sicut aedificium declinans a fundamento, disponitur ad ruinam: ita expositio mystica discrepans a sensu litterali, reputanda est indecens et inepta . . . et ideo volentibus proficere in studio sacrae Scripturae necessarium est incipere ab intellectu sensus litteralis: maxime cum ex solo sensu litterali, et non ex mystico, possit argumentum fieri ad probationem vel declarationem alicujus dubii . . .
>
> *PL* 113 Col. 29c:

> All [mystical expositions], however, presuppose the literal sense as their foundation. Therefore just as a building leaning from its foundation is in a position to fall, so a mystical exposition inconsistent with the literal sense is to be thought unsuitable and unfitting . . . and therefore it is necessary for those who wish to make progress in the study of sacred Scripture to begin from the understanding of the literal sense: especially since from the literal sense alone and not from the mystical can an argument be produced in proof or elucidation of any doubtful matter . . .

Augustine's comment on 'Thy teeth are like flocks of sheep'

(*Song of Songs*, IV, 2), that the line describes holy men, the teeth of the Church, has provoked a recent outburst of dissent from Ian Robinson who evidently thinks Augustine's view of language as capricious as Humpty Dumpty's:

> If I simply deny that these words are a description of the teeth of the church, Augustine has nothing to fall back on to convince me but authority, the naked assertion that they do mean what he says because he says so. It is hardly a parody of Augustine's position to say that anything can mean anything else, provided the church insists on it. This is not a defensible idea of language; in particular, it is not a defensible idea of poetry.[5]

Plato objects that allegorical interpretations do not necessarily protect everybody from being corrupted by the literal meanings of improper fables; Nicholas de Lyra cautions that the spiritual senses must be consonant with the literal; Ian Robinson accuses some Christian exegesis of being fanciful to the point of losing all control on meaning and communication. I want to develop in this chapter an anti-Idealist objection to allegory, almost opposite in import to Plato's. Allegory can 'spiritualise', ignore the material world, impose a 'good' interpretation (morally good, that is, from the exegete's point of view) on any story or statement. This objection might be levelled, in some form, against many allegorical works, by poets as well as critics: I think that it underlies the most personal and unresolved argument in *Piers*, the 'autobiographical episode'. The most extreme forms of allegorical procedure, in criticism or composition, may be viewed as a kind of literary Gnosticism. To read the *Song of Songs* as an expression only of Christ's love for the Church is to imply that the material world is an illusion and literal speech a smokescreen on the wall of Plato's cave. It would be possible to see the created world as a complex of analogies with divine reality and yet to think this interpretation of the *Song of Songs* a squeamish distortion of the original love poem, to feel a lack of humanity in the compulsion to allegorise. One may think that the *Song* yields naturally to interpretation as accommodated language, the words of human love being, as in many sacred poems, the only medium in which to speak of divine love. But one may feel that the spiritual interpretation denies the beauty of the literal, cleans up where nothing was dirty.

Even worse, some allegorical readings illicitly sweep under the carpet some very dirty realities. Some Christian attempts to 'spiritualise' the Old Testament make me indignant. Ian Robinson accuses St. Augustine of linguistic irresponsibility. I feel inclined to accuse some medieval comments on Scripture of moral evasiveness. For example, Rabanus Maurus 'spiritualises' the concept of usury in his commentary on the Deuteronomic prohibition on transactions at interest. Attempting to explain why the Bible allows such forbidden transactions with aliens, he cleans up the text responsible for so much prejudice and persecution:

> The 'alien' in Deuteronomy, Rabanus explains, refers to criminals and infidels. To them we give money at usury when in compensation for the expenses incurred in the preaching of the Word we demand the repentance of sins and, above all, faith together with good works. There are, in short, two meanings of the word 'money' in the passage, Rabanus concludes. To take usury for the loan of 'metallic money' is entirely forbidden; to ask usury for the offering of 'spiritual sustenance' is legitimate.[6]

The obvious objection to such exegesis is that it is special pleading. The text did mean that aliens could give and take interest and it has done harm all the way to Auschwitz. I find Rabanus's production of a more elevated meaning not only contorted but disturbingly bland. And if I am told that I lack historical sense in my reading of Rabanus, I can retort that this is precisely what he himself lacks in his dismissal of the literal meaning of a book of the Law which clearly demands to be literally obeyed.

When one refuses to make an expected imaginative translation, even parts of the New Testament can look blatantly inhumane. In *The Misery of Christianity*, Joachim Kahl's account of why he renounced his Lutheran ministry and Christian faith, he delivers a provocative attack on the parables and the teaching of St. Paul.

The parables which Jesus told according to the gospels presuppose slavery. Far from criticising it, they glorify it as a model of the relationship between God and man . . . Paul, too, not only accepted slavery as a matter of course, but even affirmed it explicitly . . . 'Everyone should remain in the state to which he was called. Were you a slave when you were called? Never mind. But if you can gain your freedom, make use of your present condition instead. For he who was called in the Lord as a slave is a freeman of the Lord. Like-wise, he who was free when called is a slave of Christ.'

I *Corinthians* VII, 20–2

Kahl's scrutiny of this passage is merciless in its literalism:

Most Christian readers of the Bible are hardly conscious of the monstrous cynicism underlying these words. By means of a verbal trick worthy of a crooked horse-dealer – giving a double meaning to the two concepts slave and freeman – those who are already oppressed are completely taken in. By virtue of the religious fiction that they are really freemen of Christ, these factual slaves are persuaded that they ought to be indifferent to their lack of freedom. Paul at the same time renames the slave-owner the slave of Christ and thus draws a veil over the existing injustice of slavery, which is justified as God's will.[7]

Kahl is probably right in claiming that most Christian readers have not responded to this passage as he does. To a reader brought up in the Christian tradition, it is more likely to seem a moving statement of the equality of men before God than a cynical piece of logic-chopping to perpetuate their inequality on earth. This may be because he has been conditioned to expect only good from the New Testament; I think that it is mainly because in reading religious literature we naturally adjust to spiritualising metaphors. He might criticise Kahl's interpretation with a Christian Platonist reply that what Kahl terms the fiction of heavenly equality is more 'real' than the fact of class distinctions of earth and makes such incongruities relatively trivial. Or, agreeing with St. Paul's anagogical sense but not with his literal advice, he

might retort that the equality of men before God proves that
they should also be equal on earth. In either case he is likely
to feel that Kahl's refusal to admit the existence of a heavenly
analogue to human society, his refusal to read metaphori-
cally, has led him to pervert the meaning of the passage into
something near its opposite.

Like the Christian reader of the New Testament, the
student of allegorical literature is usually rather docile about
making the translations expected of him. If he refuses to do
so, the text (like the passage from St. Paul which Kahl
examines) may well seem grotesque, even opposite in meaning to the allegorist's presumed intention. Part of the start-
ling effect of Angus Fletcher's *Allegory: the theory of a symbolic
mode* is that the author, while very sympathetic to allegory,
refuses to translate as much as most readers do. The book
presents an innocent-eye view of familiar allegories, an
exposure to their literally astonishing surfaces rather than to
their orthodox allegorical 'meanings'. For example, Fletcher
on *The Faerie Queene*:

> . . . the heroes in Dante and Spenser and Bunyan seem to
> create the worlds about them. They are like those people
> in real life who 'project', ascribing fictitious personalities to
> those whom they meet and live with. By analysing the
> projections, we determine what is going on in the mind of
> the highly imaginative projector . . . Redcrosse imagines
> Sansfoi and his brothers; Sir Guyon imagines Mammon
> and his cave; Sir Calidore imagines the Blatant Beast – in
> this case the subcharacters, the most numerous agents of
> an allegory, may be generated by the main protagonists,
> and the finest hero will then be the one who most
> naturally seems to generate subcharacters – aspects of
> himself – who become the means by which he is revealed,
> facet by facet. This generative function accounts for the
> frequency with which an ascetic like St Anthony is made
> the allegorical subject of both painting and literature.
> Ascetic habits produce visions of daemons, which are
> projected needs, desires and hates. This is psychologically
> a valid image of the Saint, because the state of asceticism
> with its physical debility induces extremely varied, abun-
> dant fantasies.[8]

For Fletcher allegorical personages, far from being 'frigid abstractions', are feverish monomaniacs or compulsive fantasies. The common reaction to Sir Guyon – that he boringly, smugly and safely embodies temperance and is never credibly in danger of succumbing to lust, avarice or other temptation – is the opposite of Fletcher's. His picture of Guyon as a tormented ascetic, endlessly creating temptations for himself, depends as much on a fascinated response to the literal level of *The Faerie Queene* as on a substitution of one kind of allegorical exegesis for another, modern psychoanalytic diagnosis of projection and displacement instead of traditional moral investigation of the psychomachia. If we met in actual life a person whose experience seemed limited to encountering and resisting temptations to excess, what would we think of him? What Fletcher thinks of Guyon. But there is some critical displacement in Fletcher's view of stylised fictional creations as 'like those people in real life'. His analysis of St. Anthony is in one sense winningly apt: asceticism can inflame the desires it repudiates; the troubled conscience does have a propensity to create sins. But this kind of criticism bites harder if we admit that the saints and virtues are not so presented in their fictional contexts: the analysis is more precisely of the authors and societies which produced them.

It seems unusual to respond in this way to *The Faerie Queene*. However, several critics have felt a dislocation between Langland's levels of discourse, as though *Piers Plowman* caused them particular difficulties in allegorical translation. Jay Martin's essay on the characterisation of the Dreamer as fool and wanderer discusses one example.[9] Martin argues that the *persona* of fool is appropriate for Will, placing him in the position of the wise fool who is licensed to utter disagreeable truths. Martin claims, however, that the Dreamer's role of wanderer is less successful in the argument of the poem, as this symbol associates Will with the minstrels, pilgrims and itinerant religious who are so frequently criticised on the literal level 'the restless moving class who desert their religious or political obligations for other easier or more profitable lives.' Martin's objection is that in *Piers Plowman* if someone is a wanderer in the good sense of spiritual pilgrim, he must in the mixed discourse of the narrative[10] look like a wanderer in the bad sense of vagrant; that is, that the reader will not be able to keep the literal and allegorical meanings distinct. He sums up:

> Perhaps the conflict may be expressed in this way: Langland values that which is symbolised by a wandering life or what the theologians call the *via*, the way; but when he comes to dramatise the *via* in terms of wandering, he deplores its objectification, for capricious wandering destroys the social order.

Martin's opposition of bad literal wandering and good allegorical wandering is too stark. Will is not presented as a virtuous spiritual pilgrim who, through an unfortunate choice of allegorical role, can be mistaken for a literal minstrel or derelict religious. He is accused, throughout the poem, of being like both. His wandering seems both a quest for spiritual knowledge and an indulgence of curiosity; his poverty and detachment from the world seem both disinterested and irresponsible. The 'autobiographical episode' suggests that Langland could not make up his mind about the moral status of the Dreamer's way of life. Instead of Martin's two categories (good spiritual level and bad literal level), we have at least four (good and bad spiritual states and good and bad literal actions) with compounded possibilities of confusion. And, far from being a failure in the poem, this is one of its strengths. If the 'spiritualised' version of wandering is tainted by the bad associations of literal wandering, it is because spiritual states are even harder to assess morally than literal actions. Langland refuses to simplify the problems raised by the Christian life by retreating into a purely spiritualising metaphor.

John Burrow analyses the oscillation between literal and allegorical more delicately and convincingly in his account of the second vision and its use of the symbols of pilgrimage and pardon.[11] Langland is generally opposed to literal pilgrimages. Burrow argues that Langland attempts in Passus V and VI to use the symbol of the pilgrimage polemically. The pilgrimage to Truth may represent any kind of virtuous activity but the last thing of all that it can represent is an actual pilgrimage. As if Langland feared that this might be misunderstood, he insists also on the ploughing of the half-acre and Truth finally sends the command to stay at home and continue the work. Truth, therefore, in my terms, finally refuses to endorse the 'spiritualising metaphor'. Burrow argues that the pardon is treated similarly to the pilgrimage: 'in each case there is a tension between the literal action and that which it signifies'. The granting of pardons by the Church could become a mere formality. Langland therefore resorts to the 'polemical substitution' of *Truth's* pardon, paralleling the inward pilgrimage to *Truth*. But just as the pilgrimage was first postponed and then forbidden in favour of ploughing the half-acre, so the pardon is torn in case even the symbol of true pardon may look like the dubious letter of indulgence. Langland dismantles the analogies he has created. The abandoning of Truth's pilgrimage and the tearing of Truth's pardon suggest a fear that these spiritualised images are inadequate or ambiguous: that the audience and many of the characters in the poem, like the children in Plato's *Republic*, cannot be trusted to distinguish between allegorical and literal senses.

Throughout the poem Langland is wary of the spiritualising metaphors he employs. Pardon and pilgrimage, even in their good symbolic sense, are discarded. Theology correctly interprets the heavenly meaning of Meed but misapplies the term on a crucial particular occasion. Recommendations to rely on allegorical food are qualified by their contexts: by the literal elements in the banquet scene; by the appeals to miracle and the final care for practicality of both Patience and Anima.

In *Piers Plowman and Scriptural Tradition* Robertson and Huppé seem to ignore both Langland's respect for the literal and his various scruples about the allegorical. While the traditional spiritual interpretations of Scripture are obviously relevant to *Piers*, the authors' application of them seems questionable. Their critical strategy is, in effect, to allegorise farther than Langland himself did. This is particularly striking in their treatment of the subject of food and its production. For Robertson and Huppé, ploughing consistently symbolises preaching. Piers the ploughman therefore always represents God's ministry on earth in the *status praelatorum*, a static interpretation which ignores the drama of his renun-

ciation of manual work in Passus VII and makes it symbolically equivalent to its alternative. They read the good
ploughmen of the Prologue who open the catalogue of folk
on the field as preachers: 'the food they produce must be the
spiritual life of the church',[12] although the statement that
they 'wonnen þat þise wastours with glotonye destruyeþ'
(Prologue 22) sounds determinedly literal. I think their
treatment of the Hunger episode in Passus VI a delightful
example of misplaced piety. Piers finds that only the attack
of Hunger will force the idle 'wasters' to labour but his
ravages are so pitiable that Piers begs him to compromise:
'Lat hem lyue,' he seyde, 'and lat hem ete with hogges' (VI
181). Robertson and Huppé think that the wastrels are
cowed by the withdrawal of *spiritual* food:

> Those who eat with hogs partake only of the food of the
> flesh and of the doctrines of the world . . . In other words,
> Piers threatens to excommunicate the wasters so that they
> may have no access to spiritual food, but only to the
> miserable worldly doctrines and the discomfort of sin.
> Under this threat, dissimulators go back to work . . .[13]

Such spiritual yearning and sensitivity is hardly suggested
by the language of those who say to Piers 'I was noȝt wont to
werche . . . now wol I noȝt bigynne!' (VI 167) and 'bad hym
go pissen with his plowȝ' (VI 155).[14]

Robertson and Huppé's determination to read *Piers* as a
consistent allegory of the most spiritual kind seems particularly inappropriate to the second vision. Here Langland
questions, adjusts and discards some of his own symbols,
such as ploughing, pilgrimage and pardon. Here the focus of
the poem begins to shift from man's active duties in society
towards his inner religious life, a transition obliterated by
consistently spiritual readings of food and ploughing. Piers
himself announces a change in the symbolic meaning of his
occupation: 'Of preieres and of penaunce my plouȝ shal ben
herafter' (VII 124). Of course, Langland does use spiritualising metaphors in the second vision. Like Meed, the forbidden practice of usury turns out to have a celestial analogue
for Langland as for Rabanus: '. . . beggeres borwen eueremo
and hir borgh is god almyȝty/To yelden hem þat yeueþ hem

and yet vsure moore . . .' (VII 82–3). But such spiritualising of economic terms does not totally convince in the second vision and I do not think that it is intended to. Traditionally, work and payment have been used as figures of the Christian life and its heavenly reward, as in the parable of the vineyard, to which Piers alludes at V 549–52. The first and second visions explore the relationships between the earthly and heavenly meanings of labour and reward. They attempt to establish what is just in the material world and to use the discovery analogically. But they culminate in an analogy which disturbs rather than convinces. One may believe that Truth's pardon is demonstrably valid and yet share the dismay that Piers expresses at the discovery of its formulation. 'Do yuel, and haue yuel' seems a more satisfactory maxim in the world of physical labour and survival – and even there Piers expresses doubts about it[15] – than in the sphere of eternal reward and punishment. Paradoxically, the innocent *mesure* principle is less amenable to spiritual interpretation than the villainous Meed and usury. So, in tearing the pardon and turning to a life which is not visibly or measurably productive, Piers calls into question the major analogy of the *Visio*.

Langland's dubiousness about the spiritualising metaphor is displayed most clearly – and with most self-reference – in the 'autobiographical episode' which C inserts between the first and second visions. Here the Dreamer's claim to be leading a spiritual life is questioned but neither accepted nor disproved. The placing of this interlude, between the two visions which investigate the subjects of work and economic responsibility, makes us suspicious of Will's apparent indolence. It opens:

> Thus ich awaked, god wot, whanne ich wonede on cornehulle,
> Kytte and ich in a cote cloþed as a lollere,
> And lytel y-lete by, leyue me for soþe,
> Among lollares of london and lewede heremytes;
> For ich made of þo men as reson me tauhte.
> For as ich cam by conscience with reson ich mette
> In an hote heruest whenne ich hadde myn hele,
> And lymes to labore with and louede wel fare,

And no dede to do bote drynke and to slepe.
In hele and in vnite on me aposede;
Romynge in remembraunce thus reson me aratede.

C VI 1–11

The criticism of the Dreamer is obvious: he is able-bodied, sound of mind,[16] has a wife to support and is living in poverty in a 'cote'. The season is harvest, literally a time when extra labourers are needed, symbolically the moment when achievement comes to the full and is judged. Yet Will not only wastes time, sleeps and drinks, behaves and looks like a loller, but has the self-righteousness to compose satirical poems about lollers. He claims that in doing so he is following the command of Reason, but he seems to have missed the personal application which Reason now forces upon him. When Reason rebukes him and asks why he cannot work, he has a variety of excuses: that he is too weak, too tall, that he does not enjoy any tasks except clerkly occupations, and that in the Bible clerks are excused from 'knauene werkes' (C VI 12–62).

The Dreamer's vindication of himself seems to slide between an embarrassed parade of admittedly inadequate excuses and an attempt to assert the primacy of the spiritual. 'Ich am. . . to long, leyf me, lowe for to stoupe' (C VI 23–4) sounds like a bid to turn the whole subject into a joke, the sort of thing Falstaff might say if he were, *per impossibile*, thin, earnest and religious. Yet this spiritualising metaphor constitutes a serious defence of his way of life:

The lomes þat ich laboure with and lyflode deserue
Ys *pater-noster* and my prymer *placebo and dirige*,
And my sauter som tyme and my seuene psalmes.

C VI 45–7

In form and content this resembles Piers's announcement, 'Of preieres and of penaunce my plou3 shal ben herafter' (VII 124), which seems above suspicion. Yet it is not clear that the Dreamer has earned the right to use the metaphor, that his life provides a literal level consistent with such an allegory. It is ambiguous whether he expresses faith or irresponsibility in quoting the texts assuring us that God will provide which sound somewhat unrealistic even from the mouth of Patience:

> 'Non de solo, ich seide, 'for soþe uiuit homo
> Nec in pane & pabulo þe pater-noster witnesseþ;
> Fiat uoluntas tua fynt ous alle þynges.'
>
> C VI 86–8

Later in C 'on heihte actif, an hosebounde semed' (C VIII 299) will be implicitly condemned for pleading matrimony, 'Ich may nat come for a kytte' (C VIII 304), and refusing to follow Piers. But here Will's failure to provide adequately for his 'kytte' is questioned. Can someone so involved in active life be deemed a contemplative and dismiss all practical concerns? And is his contemplation genuine or escapist?

The response of the Dreamer's interlocutors, Conscience and Reason, to his apologia seems a baffled one. They could define Meed, direct the King and set the country on the right path in the previous vision, but they seem unable to assess the spiritual condition of an apparent idler and alleged contemplative who defends himself with the authority of Scripture. Conscience's reply to the Dreamer's battery of texts sounds puzzled:

> Quath conscience, 'by crist ich can nat see this lyeþ;
> Ac it semeth nouht parfytnesse in cytees for to begge,
> Bote he be obediencer to pryour oþer to mynstre.'
>
> C VI 89–91

Conscience feels that there is something wrong with the Dreamer's defence of himself but he seems unable to analyse what it is. He can issue the fairly obvious rebuff that the only mendicants should be members of religious orders, who have made a solemn commitment to renounce the world, to follow perfection, and have not encumbered themselves, as has Will, with such responsibilities as marriage. Yet the form of his reply with its institutional words 'obediencer', 'pryour', 'mynstre', following the mystical anarchy of the Dreamer's Latin texts, suggests more than a practical objection to casual parasites on society. Conscience is asking for something

objective, a literal level in the Dreamer's life which would
provide evidence about the spiritual level.

The Dreamer, growing more confident, concludes with a
passionate assertion of the spiritualising metaphor, a statement of faith, supported by the Biblical parables of the
hidden treasure and the lost coin, in heavenly riches which
do not conform to any earthly laws of economics:

> 'That ys soth,' ich seide, 'and so ich by-knowe,
> That ich haue tynt tyme and tyme mysspended;
> And ȝut, ich hope, as he þat oft haueþ chaffared,
> Pat ay hath lost and lost and atte last hym happed
> He bouhte suche a bargayn he was þe bet euere,
> And sette hus lost at a lef at þe last ende,
> Such a wynnynge hym warth þorw wordes of hus grace;
>> *Simile est regnum celorum thesauro abscondito in agro,*
>> *& cetera;*
>> *Mulier que inuenit dragmam unam, et cetera;*
> So hope ich to haue of hym þat is al-myghty
> A gobet of hus grace and bygynne a tyme,
> Pat alle tymes of my tyme to profit shal turne.'
>
> C VI 92–101

Conscience and Reason leave the matter in abeyance, merely
uttering good advice in the vaguest possible terms:

> 'Ich rede þe,' quath reson þo, 'rape þe to by-gynne
> Pe lyf þat is lowable and leel to þe soule' –
> 'Ȝe and continue;' quath conscience . . .
>
> C VI 102–4

Neither does anything to define what, in the Dreamer's case,
this righteous life would be.

Perhaps Langland did not know either. At least one aspect
of the problem never gets clearly defined in this episode: that
the Dreamer is talking about poetry but thinks that he is
talking about prayer. The closest he comes to formulating his
anxieties about his poem is, characteristically, on the subject
of satire: Reason both teaches him to criticise lollers and
accuses him of being a loller himself. Yet, even if Will's work
were entirely prayer and questions about the value of poetry

were excluded, would the problems raised in this episode be soluble? How can anyone's spiritual condition be assessed, even – or especially – by himself? How can one tell whether the spiritualising metaphor expresses divine inspiration or irresponsible self-deception?

Yet the spiritualising metaphor is the basis of any Christian allegorical work. Will's dialogue with Imaginatif in B asks 'What is the poem for?' The conversation with Reason and Conscience implies the question 'What does the poem mean?' or 'How does the poem mean?' And the form of the allegory itself suggests that we can never definitively know. Reason and Conscience, looking doubly allegorical in the context of the waking interlude, are Will's critics but also his creations. They do not give a final answer but, if they did, it would be Will's answer. Or, even if we prefer not to read the episode as 'autobiographical', it would be Langland's answer. And the religious poet can do no more than offer 'hints and guesses' in the human language available to him. Piers – we are to believe – could offer more, but the poem which creates him cannot. It gestures towards him and the Truth which he expresses. It can conclude only in the search for him.

# Notes

Books and articles mentioned more than once are, after full reference has been given, cited by author and short title.

Quotations from the A and B texts of *Piers Plowman* are from *Piers Plowman: the A Version* ed. George Kane (London, 1960) and *Piers Plowman: the B Version* ed. George Kane and E. Talbot Donaldson (London, 1975). Quotations from the C text are from the E.E.T.S. edition, *The Vision of William concerning Piers the Plowman, together with Vita de Dowel, Dobet, et Dobest, secundum Wit et Resoun* ed. W. W. Skeat (London, 1867–84). Where not otherwise identified, references are to the B version.

## INTRODUCTION

1. Single authorship is now generally accepted. For a brief account of the earlier controversy about multiple authorship, see Morton W. Bloomfield, 'The Present State of *Piers Plowman* Studies', *Speculum*, XIV (1939), 215–32. David Fowler has since argued that A and B are by different authors (*Piers the Plowman: Literary Relations of the A- and B-Texts*, Seattle, 1961) but his views have had little influence. Most recent critics of *Piers* have been confirmed in their impression of single authorship by the logic and precision of George Kane's *Piers Plowman: The Evidence for Authorship* (London, 1965). E. T. Donaldson's masterly analysis of the C version, *Piers Plowman: the C- Text and its Poet* (Yale, 1949), provides additional evidence for supposing that B and C are by the same poet.
2. In Chapter 5 I shall consider the relevance to *Piers* of the tradition of negative theology and the value placed on the allegorical obscurity of the Bible. For a densely theological exposition of a deliberate riddle in *Piers*, see R. E. Kaske, '"Ex vi transicionis" and its Passage in *Piers Plowman*', *JEGP*, LXII (1963), 32–60.
3. See Donaldson, *Piers: C-Text*, 199–226: 'The Poet: Biographical Material'.
4. See Kane, *Authorship*, 28–70.
5. Kane, *Authorship*, 52–70.

6. The most extreme proponents of this view are D. W. Robertson, Jr. and Bernard Huppé in *Piers Plowman and Scriptural Tradition* (Princeton, 1951), e.g. 'when the name Will is first introduced . . . it is accompanied by a play on its meaning as the faculty of will. This play on the name of the dreamer and his character as it is developed in the poem together suggest that the dreamer is representative of the faculty will rather than of any individual person', 34.

7. Aquinas defines the will as an appetitive rather than a rational faculty (*Summa Theologia* 1ª Q. LXXXII). The *Sentences* of Peter Lombard, one of the most influential theological text books at this period, repeat an Augustinian definition of the soul: that it is composed of will, memory and understanding, resembling the Trinity in its three-fold nature (PL 192 Col. 512, derived from *De Trinitate*, X 11–12). Langland is fond of thinking in triads: in so far as the narrator is a personification of the will, his relationships to Imaginatif and to the hypostatisations of learning and understanding in *Dowel* fit neatly into the Augustinian scheme. But, in his predominant intellectual curiosity, Will seems to overlap this definition of *voluntas*. Donaldson discusses the Bernardine concept of free will in relation to the character *Liberum Arbitrium* in C (*Piers: C-Text*, 183–96). He demonstrates the importance of the concept in the poem but it is essential to remember that *Liberum Arbitrium* has replaced Piers in this episode and is more closely associated with him than with Will.

8. For argument from etymology, especially as applied to names, see K. K. Ruthven, *The Conceit* (London, 1969), 38–41: 'Every *nomen* conceals an *omen*' (p. 38). Langland uses argument from etymology at XV 448–51 when he (correctly) derives 'heathen' from 'heath' – 'Heþen is to mene after heeþ and vntiled erþe' (XV 459) – and implicitly relates its original meaning to the spiritual sense of one of the poem's dominant metaphors, agriculture. Langland also shows his interest in the meaning of names when Will questions Conscience on the distinction between 'Christ' and 'Jesus' (XIX 15–25).

9. See especially Sonnets CXXXV, CXXXVI.

10. The dream is not explicitly concluded, no matter where one thinks John But's addition begins. This is one of the strongest reasons for believing A an unfinished poem. For the view that 'the dreamer awakens at this point' and 'the poem comes to an emphatic conclusion', see Knott and Fowler, *Piers the Plowman: A Critical Edition of the A-Version* (Baltimore, 1952) 169, note on A XI 250.

11. The best literary introduction to the subject of typology is Erich Auerbach 'Figura' in *Scenes from the Drama of European Literature* (New York, 1959), 11–76. 'Figura' in literature derives from the typological thought which connects, for example, the crossing of the Red Sea with the sacrament of baptism and the person of Adam with Christ. In Auerbach's terms, it differs from 'allegory' in that neither of the corresponding elements is fictional. Theological allegory can be seen in facts as much as in words.

12. For example, by Goethe:

> Es [*Symbolism*] *ist die Sache, ohne die Sache zu sein, und doch die Sache; ein im geistigen Spiegel zusammengezogenes Bild, und doch mit dem Gegenstand identisch. Wie weit steht nicht dagegen Allegorie zurück; sie ist vielleicht*

*geistreich witzig, aber doch meist rhetorisch und konventionell und immer besser, je mehr sie sich demjenigen nähert, was wir Symbol nennen*
Goethe, *Geaenkausgabe der Werke, Briefe und Gespräche*

(Zurich, 1949), 13

On this view symbolism is almost mystical in its perception of unity in apparent diversity; allegory, however, is a mere rhetorical gesture deriving more from convention than from insight. See also *Maximen*, where Goethe argues that in allegory the poet uses the particular only as example of the general, whereas in symbolism the particular is a revelation of the general. Coleridge probably follows Goethe in regarding allegory as primarily satisfying the intellect and symbolism as more deeply truthful and unified, claiming that an allegory must be consciously constructed whereas a symbol may be spontaneously drawn from subconscious knowledge:

> The advantage of symbolic writing over allegory is, that it presumes no disjunction of faculties, but simple dominance. (*Miscellaneous Criticism*, 29).
> We may then safely define allegorical writing as the employment of one set of agents and images with actions and accompaniments correspondent, so as to convey, while in disguise, either moral qualities or conceptions of the mind that are not in themselves objects of the senses, or other images, agents, actions, fortunes, and circumstances so that *the difference is everywhere presented to the eye or imagination while the likeness is suggested to the mind* [my italics]
> (*Miscellaneous Criticism*, 30)

These distinctions made by Goethe and Coleridge are, presumably, the ancestors of the formulation by C. S. Lewis of allegory as a 'habit of expression' and symbolism as a 'habit of thought' in *The Allegory of Love* (Oxford, 1936), 47–8. Lewis, however, clearly has more affection and respect for allegory than do Goethe and Coleridge. For a consideration of the inconsistencies in Lewis's account of allegory and symbolism, see A. D. Nuttall, *Two Concepts of Allegory* (Barnes and Noble, 1967) Chapter II. For a discussion of allegory which not only condemns any rigid demarcation from symbolism but also dazzles the reader to seeing allegorical and literal as one, see Angus Fletcher's *Allegory: the Theory of a Symbolic Mode* (Cornell, 1964).
13. For example, Robertson and Huppé, *Scriptural Tradition*.

CHAPTER 1

1. 'The Tearing of the Pardon', *Piers Plowman: Critical Approaches*, ed. S. S. Hussey (London, 1969), 52.
2. T. P. Dunning suggests in *Piers Plowman: an Interpretation of the A-text*

(Dublin, 1937) that Piers's anger is with himself. He learns that, like Martha, he has been too concerned with the practical, with ploughing rather than pilgrimage. In a later study, 'The Structure of the B-Text of *Piers Plowman*, *RES*, N. S., VII (1956), 225–37, Dunning argues that, because of the pardon, Piers 'moves from the *animale* to the *spirituale*'.

In 'An Interpretation of the A-text of *Piers Plowman*', *PMLA*, LIII (Sept. 1938), 656–77, G. W. Stone reads the scene in almost the opposite sense. In his view, the pardon commands Piers to continue in his previous labours and Piers, who had expected respite and commendation, is understandably – but culpably – disappointed:

> It [the pardon] commanded Piers to keep on working if he would be saved. Piers is an idealist and a very human one. He thought he had finished his work. He thought in his old age to supplant fifteen years of active service to Truth with a period of contemplation of Truth. He had hoped for some honourable mention concerning the deeds he had performed. To receive this simple and stark command when he had expected so much more seems hard. Even the best of humans, the dreamer learns, backslide, for Piers in pure anger tears the pardon asunder and in his bitterness makes a speech in which he declares he will not work in the future the hard way he has in the past.

Most recent interpretations, even if their emphasis and treatment of detail are various, see in the tearing of the pardon a mysterious figure of the Atonement and the transition from the Old Law to the New. In 'The Pardon of Piers Plowman', *Proceedings of the British Academy*, XXX (1944), 303–57, Nevill Coghill argues that the statement that Truth 'purchased' the pardon is virtually synonymous with the doctrine that Christ 'bought' (redeemed) mankind. The pardon, therefore, of which Piers sees the spirit but the priest merely the letter, stands for the Atonement. But Coghill finds its expression, though a quotation from the Athanasian Creed, 'grim' and 'threatening' and thinks Piers then confronts the problem that, if all are sinful, none can deserve salvation through 'doing well'. On this view, the pardon confronts us with the harshness of the Old Law and suggests its resolution in the New.

John Lawlor's interpretation ('The Pardon Scene in *Piers Plowman*', *Speculum* XXVI (1951), 317–31), though described by Rosemary Woolf as almost the reverse of Coghill's, actually has a good deal in common with it: the strict justice implied in the wording of the pardon would condemn even Piers, since no one is absolutely good. In tearing the pardon, Piers implores mercy.

Rosemary Woolf, while thinking these interpretations almost opposite, proposes an interesting solution consistent with both: the medieval audience would have responded to the 'pardon' as a condemnation, but the tearing of a condemnation constitutes a reprieve or pardon ('The Tearing of the Pardon'), (Hussey, *Critical Approaches*).

Mary Schroeder (Mary Carruthers) argues that the tearing of the pardon alludes to the smashing of the tablets of the Law by Moses in *Exodus* XXXII, 19. An exegetical tradition makes the breaking of the tablets a type of the change from the Old Law to the New; the tearing of the pardon heralds a transition from the world of the *Visio*, based on 'measurable hire' rather than grace, to the New Covenant and the possibility of redeemed nature ('*Piers Plowman*: the Tearing of the Pardon', *PQ*, XLIX (Jan. 1970), 8–18). A connection between the tearing of the pardon and the smashing of the tablets had earlier been suggested by Howard Meroney who also sees the Piers of the *Visio* as representative of the limitations of the Old Testament, 'a ridiculous Adam-Moses' ('The Life and Death of Longe Wille', *ELH*, XVII (1950), 1–35).

Several critics have emphasised the clash between the form and the content of the pardon, its meaning and value obscured by the fact that it looks like a letter of indulgence. This view is adumbrated by R. W. Chambers in *Man's Unconquerable Mind* (London, 1939), 119. It was formulated most clearly and influentially by R. W. Frank, *Piers Plowman and the Scheme of Salvation* (New Haven, 1957), Ch. 3. The scene is read similarly by J. A. W. Burrow in 'The Action of Langland's Second Vision', *EC*, XV (1965), 247–68, and Ian Bishop, *Pearl in its Setting* (Oxford, 1968), 64–5.

3. From Truth in B and C; from Truth and the Pope in A.

4. Frank, *Scheme of Salvation*, 28.

5. As far as I know, the only critic who considers it a completed poem is David Fowler, *Literary Relations*.

6. See Knott and Fowler, *A-Version*, 169.

In the C version Langland is careless on one occasion about telling us that the Dreamer has woken. See R. W. Frank, 'The Number of Visions in *Piers Plowman*', *MLN*, LVI (May, 1951), 309–12.

7. This explanation is an obvious concomitant of belief in single author-ship. R. W. Chambers advanced it when the authorship controversy was at its height: 'In this conclusion of A no attempt whatever is made to solve the problems the dreamer has raised. Could a stranger ending be devised? . . . The obvious explanation is that the poet could not devise a satisfactory answer to the questions he had asked . . . Not often has the struggle of a poet's soul during a longer series of years been told as it is in these first two passus of the *B-continuation*.' 'Long Will, Dante and the Righteous Heathen', *Essays and Studies by Members of the English Association* IX (Oxford, 1924), 54, 58. Re-stated almost *verbatim* in *Man's Unconquerable Mind*, 130, 149.

8. For discussion and definition of Imaginatif, see H. S. V. Jones, 'Imaginatif in Piers Plowman', *JEGP*, XIII (1914), 583–88; Randolph Quirk, '*Vis Imaginativa*', *JEGP*, LIIII (1954), 81–3; Morton W. Bloomfield, *Piers Plowman as a Fourteenth-Century Apocalypse* (New Brunswick, 1962), Appendix III, 170–4.

9. In Skeat's edition the phrase occurs in the same form at Prologue 19 and XIX 225. Kane and Donaldson's reading of the later line is 'To wynne wiþ truþe þat þe world askeþ' (XIX 230).

10. T. D. Whitaker *Visio Willi de Petro Plouhman, Item Visiones ejusdem de Dowel, Dobet, et Dobest* (London, 1813). Notes, 16, and Introduction, XXX. Quoted and slightly re-worded by Skeat.

11. For example, Robertson and Huppé, *Scriptural Tradition*.

12. *Robert Crowley, The Vision of Pierce Plowman* (London, 1550), the first printed edition of the poem. Langland's criticisms of the medieval Church were evidently welcome after the Reformation. In this edition they are emphasised by polemical marginal notes. For example, at II 115 Theology is described, in an obviously anti-clerical gloss, as 'the true preacher'. Meed's promise of a stained glass window in return for absolution by the friar (III 48–63) provokes the comment: 'The fruites of popische penaunce'. The specific satirical targets rather than the general moral import of Wrath's confession are underlined by the note on V 153: 'Nunnes'.

13. Charles Muscatine, 'Locus of Action in Medieval Narrative', *RP*, XVII (August, 1963), 115–22.

14. Charles Muscatine, *Chaucer and the French Tradition* (Berkeley, 1957).

15. Elizabeth Salter, '*Piers Plowman* and the Visual Arts', *Encounters* ed. John Dixon Hunt (London, 1971), 11–27.

16. Bloomfield, *Apocalypse*, 19.

17. It often goes with an optimistic 'Christian' reading. Another example is Edward Vasta, *The Structure of Piers Plowman* (Hague, 1965), which seems, especially in Chapters 3 and 8, to idealise Will very uncritically and claims that by the end of the poem he has achieved perfection.

18. Salter, 'Visual Arts'.

19. Robertson and Huppé, *Scriptural Tradition*.

20. Bloomfield, *Apocalypse*.

21. I use the term 'Christian' to describe not the religious beliefs or commitments of these scholars but their critical approach to medieval literature.


CHAPTER 2

1. Among them: Whitaker, *Piers*, Notes 16 and Introduction XXX; B. Ten Brink, *History of English Literature*, tr. H. M. Kennedy, (New York, 1863), I, 365; W. J. Courthope, *History of English Poetry* (London, 1919), I, 226; H. W. Wells, *PMLA*, XLIV (1929), 127; H. W. Troyer, *PMLA*, XLVII (1932), 378; Stone, 'Interpretation of A-text', 677; C. Dawson, *Medieval Religion and other Essays* (New York, 1934), 162–3; G. H. Gerould, 'The Structural Integrity of *Piers Plowman*', *SP*, XLV (1948), 60–75; R. W. Chambers, *Essays and Studies*, and *Man's Unconquerable Mind*; Muscatine, 'Locus of Action'.

2. Mary Carruthers, *The Search for Saint Truth* (Evanston, 1973), 172.

3. Robertson and Huppé, *Scriptural Tradition*; Salter, 'Visual Arts'.

4. E. T. Donaldson, in *MLN*, LXVIII (1953), 141–2, reviewing Sister Rose Bernard Donna, *Despair and Hope: a Study in Langland and Augustine* (Washington, D.C., 1948).

5. In C there is some revision of names so that the sins are more consistently abstract. 'Pernele proud-herte' becomes 'pruyde' (C VII 14); 'Lechour' becomes 'lecherie' (C VII 170); 'glotoun', however, remains in the more particular form.

6. William Jordan, O. P. See M. E. Marcett, *Uthred de Boldon, Friar William Jordan and Piers Plowman* (New York, 1938).

7. A subject discussed by Constance B. Hieatt in *The Realism of Dream Visions* (Hague, 1967). She suggests a psychological explanation:

> There may . . . be a real justification for the inclusion of these scenes in
> the poet's waking, rather than dreaming, life. Metaphorical as they are,
> they refer very specifically to the immediate, physical, personal circum-
> stances of the poet's life. That he encountered Need is another way of
> saying that he was 'metelees and monelees'. These personal concerns
> only appear in a much larger context within the dreams; there the
> dreamer is concerned with the myriad implications for all mankind of
> need and poverty, not just with his own poverty. The waking se-
> quences, then, provide a personal motivation for the visions which
> follow . . . (94).

8. Opinions on Need's advice vary. It is approved by Bloomfield,
*Apocalypse*, 135–7, and Robertson and Huppé, *Scriptural Tradition*, 227–9. It
is questioned by Frank, *Scheme of Salvation*, 113–14, and Carruthers, *Search*,
160–2.
9. See Frank, 'The Number of Visions'.
10. The concept of 'figura' as the most factual kind of allegory is obviously
of immense importance here. See Auerbach, 'Figura'.
11. Frank, *Scheme of Salvation*, 34.
12. For example, Wells, 'Structure of the B-Text'; Coghill, 'The Pardon';
Donaldson, *Piers: C-Text*, 156–61, who suggests various interpretations of
the triad but cautions 'I think we err when we try to pin the poet down to
any single system of theological thinking' (159).
13. David Mills, 'The Role of the Dreamer', Hussey, *Critical Approaches*,
180–212; Anne Middleton, 'Two Infinites: Grammatical Metaphor in *Piers
Plowman*', *ELH*, XXXIV (June, 1972), 169–88.
14. Middleton, 'Infinites'.
15. Fowler, *Literary Relations*: 'his questions are often loaded and his
ignorance is Swiftian', 18.
16. A connection made elsewhere in the poem: XI 413–19; XV 48–51.
17. A view proposed by Greta Hort, *Piers Plowman and Contemporary
Religious Thought* (London, 1938): 'The Dreamer's abrupt request to Holy
Church to be taught to know falsehood is in keeping with the best
tradition; it is not prompted by idle curiosity . . . It was the legitimate and
necessary question of a man who held that a knowledge of both truth and
falsehood was necessary for right living and thinking.' (61). She quotes, as
evidence of this tradition, from Abelard's *Dialectica*:

> 'All knowledge is good, even that which relates to evil, because a
> righteous man must have it. Since he must guard against evil, it is
> necessary that he should know it beforehand: otherwise he could not
> shun it. Though an act be evil, knowledge regarding it is good; though
> it be evil to sin, it is good to know the sin, which otherwise we could
> not shun . . .' (60).

18. Robertson and Huppé, *Scriptural Tradition*, who consider the poem
strongly anti-fraternal in emphasis, object that the friars err in the spirit, if
not the letter, of their advice (101–2). Carruthers, *Search*, 86, complains
that 'given Will's initial misunderstanding of Dowel', the form of the

friars' explanation misleads him further. Most critics of the poem, however, accept their distinction between venial and mortal sin as valid and
their allegory as loosely appropriate.

19. See Burrow, 'Action of the Second Vision'.

20. Donaldson, *Piers: C-Text*, 163.

21. Donaldson, *Piers: C-Text*, 166.

22. A. C. Spearing, 'Verbal Repetition in *Piers Plowman* B and C', *JEGP*,
LXII, (October, 1963), 722–37.

23. Burke, *On the Sublime and the Beautiful*, Section VIII.

24. For a collection of such theological statements, see Ian Ramsey, *Words
about God*, (Guildford and London, 1971).

25. *Symposium*, 201D–12A; 216B.

## CHAPTER 3

1. Gabriel Josipovici, *The World and the Book* (London, 1971).

2. Muscatine, *Chaucer*, gives a detailed and sensitive analysis of the
implications of style in *Troilus*.

3. Carruthers, *Search*, investigates the language of the poem in terms of
corrupt and redeemed speech. She claims that 'analysis of words as
ambiguous tools of thought, capable not only of revealing a true cognition
but also of generating a corruption of understanding, is the basic concern
of the poem' (4).

4. Donaldson, *Piers: C-Text*, 136–55.

5. Some of the material of Hawkin's speech in B is distributed among the
Deadly Sins in C. This, perhaps, has the effect of making the condemnation of the abuses even more general.

6. Suggested as a possible source for Piers's 'tene' at the pardon by
Schroeder (Carruthers), 'The Tearing of the Pardon', and Meroney,
'Longe Wille'.

7. John Peter, *Complaint and Satire in Early English Literature* (Oxford, 1956).

8. Ibid., 21, 29.

9. Ibid., 5–6.

10 Ibid., 56, 76, 78, 94, 95.

## CHAPTER 4

1. Lewis, *Allegory of Love*, 15, 29.

2. 'The Life of Milton', *Lives of the Poets* (Oxford, 1905), I, 185.

3. Fletcher, *Allegory*, 29n.

4. From *Medieval English Lyrics* ed. Theodore Silverstein (London, 1971),
53.

5. Skeat reads: 'to þe plow'.

6. Skeat's reading, 'lappe', equally suggests a pun on an erotic sense.

7. Skeat reads: 'Plededen for penyes and poundes þe lawe' (Prologue
212). Even if 'poundes' is based on a scribal error, the misunderstanding
presumably arose from the word play in 'pounded': the lawyers *expounded*

the law for *pounds*.

8. Another example of the moral danger in the ambiguities of language. Life is the more easily misled since 'hende' ranges in meaning from 'courteous' in the best sense to 'expedient'. Chaucer exploits the ambiguity of the word for comic purposes in *The Miller's Tale*.

9. For an analysis of the relevant associations of 'plante', see P. M. Kean, 'Langland on the Incarnation', *RES*, NS XVI (1965), 349–63.

10. See Michael Baxandall, *Painting and Experience in Fifteenth-Century Italy* (Oxford, 1972), 43. Baxandall quotes from St. Antonino, Archbishop of Florence: 'Painters are to be blamed when they paint things contrary to our Faith . . . when they paint the infant Jesus with a hornbook, even though he never learned from man.'

11. Possibly the lines 'Til he weex a faunt þoruȝ hir flessh and of fightyng koupe/To haue yfouȝte wiþ þe fend er ful tyme come' (XVI 101–2) also subsume the image of a natural child's pugnacity into the theology of the battle with evil. Compare Empson's controversial analysis of Herbert's line 'Man stole the fruit but I must climb the tree' in *Seven Types of Ambiguity* (London, 1930; revised edition, 1947), 232.

12. Carruthers, *Search*, thinks that the poem as a whole criticises personification allegory in favour of figural allegory as a superior mode of cognition. On this view, Wit's description, though not exactly incorrect, encourages the Dreamer in a misleading habit of thought to which he is already prone.


CHAPTER 5

1. For a brief account of the *Consolation* and the reasons for thinking Boethius's Christian beliefs deliberately excluded from it, see C. S. Lewis, *The Discarded Image* (Cambridge, 1964), 75–91.

2. For a discussion of how this idea relates in detail to *Piers*, see Barbara Raw, 'Piers and the Image of God in Man' in Hussey, *Critical Approaches*, 143–79.

3. See Auerbach, 'Figura'.

4. For a brief and lucid exposition of the importance of this cosmology for medieval literature, see Josipovici, *The World and The Book*, Chapter 2.

5. C XX 25–45.

6. One may feel this about Langland's 'proof' that the poor do not feel covetous, since poverty is small, covetousness large and it is no fun for unequally matched partners to fight together (XIV 239–44). My favourite inappropriate figure is Aristaeus in Henryson's *Orpheus and Eurydice*. In the fable, he threatens to assault Eurydice and she runs away; in the allegorical interpretation, Aristaeus proves to represent Virtue and Eurydice is condemned for fleeing its attractions. The emotional incongruity is defended by John MacQueen, *Robert Henryson* (Oxford, 1967): 'He [Aristaeus] is a ravisher, whose allegorical function as Virtue is combined with his literal role in a stylistic yoking of apparent incompatibles very characteristic of medieval allegory, and with an effect not dissimilar to that of later metaphysical imagery.' (34).

7. R. P. Blackmur, *A Primer of Ignorance* (New York, 1967), 43.

8. Their names are not only ambiguous but unstable: at IV 67 the Christian name has shifted from one to the other, 'Wisdom and sire waryn þe witty'; by IV 76 they have become 'Wisdom and witte'.

9. For an analysis of the C addition, see A. G. Mitchell, 'Lady Meed and the Art of *Piers Plowman*' (London, 1956). For the significance of grammatical imagery in *Piers*, see Middleton' 'Infinites'.

10. Prologue to *Morall Fabillis*, Robert Henryson, *Poems*, ed. Charles Elliott (Oxford, 1963), 1. In the third stanza I prefer the reading 'sueit and delectabill' of the Bannatyne MS to the Oxford text 'and is dellectabill'. Henryson surely intends to present a sharp contrast between the sensory qualities of the hard shell and the sweet kernel.

11. J. W. H. Atkins, *English Literary Criticism: the Medieval Phase* (Cambridge, 1943), 46–9.

12. Ibid., 20.

13. Ian Bishop, *Pearl in its Setting* (Oxford, 1968).

14. Ibid., 71.

15. Ibid., 63.

16. Skeat's spelling 'redeles' (XIII 184) suggests a pun: 'read redeless'. Clergy sneers at Conscience both for reading 'riddles' and for presuming to read 'without instruction'.

17. The image derives from *The Consolation of Philosophy* II m 8. For another and more elaborate version in Middle English poetry, see *The Knight's Tale*, CT I 2987–3040.

18. I have modified the punctuation of Migne's *Patrologia Latina*.

## CHAPTER 6

1. I perhaps simplify Frank's position, which is stated in *Scheme of Salvation*, 2–3, and explained more fully in 'The Art of Reading Medieval Personification – Allegory', *ELH*, XX (1953), 237–50. However, his view of the status of an allegorical character is significantly different from my own. A small minority of critics of *Piers* have considered the co-existence of the modes. Muscatine notes the 'alternation of allegory and literalism' as contributing to the 'insecurity of . . . structure' but finds the effect random rather than purposeful ('Locus of Action'). Two recent studies give sensitive accounts of the fictional variety of the Prologue: Elizabeth Kirk, *The Dream Thought of Piers Plowman* (New Haven and London, 1972), 15–28, and Carruthers, *Search*, 26–33.

2. Whitaker's note on C XXIII 359.

3. Lewis, *Allegory of Love*, 47–8.

## CHAPTER 7

1. *Jubilate Agno*, VII.

2. CT, X, 48–51; 'The Retreat'.

3. The New English Bible conveys more the sense of *solliciti* than the

translation 'Take no thought for your life' of the Authorised Version. For Langland the obvious translation of *solliciti* was 'bisy' (VII 123, 130).

4. *Matthew* XIX 16–22; Donaldson, *Piers: C-Text*, 160–1.

5. Donaldson, *Piers: C-Text*, 164.

6. Ibid., 167–8.

7. *PL* 114 Col. 530d.

8. Recklessness is interestingly discussed by Donaldson, *Piers: C-Text*, 171–5. I follow Skeat and Donaldson in assigning C XIII 88–XIV 128 to Recklessness.

9. The Bull of John XXII, *Cum inter nonnullos*, in 1323 declared it heresy to assert that Christ and the Apostles had not owned any property. For a brief discussion on the controversy, see W. A. Pantin, *The English Church in the Fourteenth Century* (Cambridge, 1955), 123–4.

10. Bloomfield, *Apocalypse*, 72.

11 See J. A. W. Burrow, 'Words, Works and Will' in Hussey, *Critical Approaches*.

## CHAPTER 8

1. e.g. Xenophanes. See W. K. Guthrie, *History of Greek Philosophy* (Cambridge, 1962), I, 360ff.

2. See Marcel Simon, *Hercule et le christianisme* (Paris, 1955) and Domenico Comparetti, *Vergil in the Middle Ages*, trans. E. F. M. Benecke (New York and London, 1895), 96–118.

3. This is the interpretation consistently provided in the *Glossa Ordinaria*:

Ubi per epithalamium carmen conjunctionem Christi et Ecclesie mystice canit . . . Omnes animae motiones universitatis conditor Deus creavit ad bonum: sed usu nostro saepe fit ut res quae per naturam bonae sunt, dummale his abutimur, nos ad peccatum deducant. Unus ex animae motibus amor est, quo bene utimur si sapientiam amemus, et veritatem: Male autem si carnem et sanguinem. Tu igitur ut spiritualis audi spiritualiter amatoria verba cantici cantari, et disce motum animae tuae et naturalis amoris incendium ad meliora transferre (*PL* 133 Col. 1127a 1127d):

Where the union of Christ and the Church is mystically celebrated through the wedding song . . . God, the maker of the universe, created all the motions of the soul towards the good; but it often happens because of our use that things which are by nature good lead us towards sin when we evilly abuse them. One of the affections of the soul is love, which we use well if we love wisdom and truth but badly if we love flesh and blood. Therefore, as a spiritual being, listen in a spiritual way to the amorous language of the song and learn to transfer the passion of your soul and the fire of natural love to better things.

4. *Republic*, trans. Cornford (Oxford, 1941) 68–9.

5. Ian Robinson, *Chaucer and the English Tradition* (Cambridge, 1972), 173.

6. Benjamin N. Nelson, *The Idea of Usury* (Princeton, 1949), 5. He is summarising Rabanus's comments in *Enarratio super Deuteronium (PL* 108, Col. 946–7).

7. Joachim Kahl, *The Misery of Christianity* (London, 1972), 28–9.

8. Fletcher, *Allegory*, 35–6.

9. Jay Martin, 'Wil as Fool and Wanderer in *Piers Plowman'*, *Texas Studies in Literature and Language* III no. 4 (Winter, 1962), 535–48.

10. Martin does not specifically draw attention to this feature of the poem but his argument depends upon it.

11. Burrow, 'Action of Second Vision'.

12. Robertson and Huppé, *Scriptural Tradition*, 19.

13. Ibid., 84–5.

14. Langland seems to discourage an exclusively 'spiritual' reading of the Hunger episode in omitting in C the lines:

> Kynde wit wolde þat ech wiȝt wroȝte,
> Or wiþ techynge or tellynge or trauaillyng of hondes,
> Contemplatif lif or Actif lif; crist wolde it als.

VI 247–9

The revision of this passage is discussed by A. C. Spearing, 'The Development of a theme in *Piers Plowman'*, *RES*, N. S. XI (August, 1960), 241–53. Spearing also disagrees with the reading of Robertson and Huppé and suggests that 'C's aim is that Hunger should preach a doctrine of labour in a purely material sense'.

15. VI 199–211.

16. An alternative MS reading to 'unite' (C VI 10) is 'inwitte'. This is more intelligible and reinforces the point that the Dreamer is sound in both body and mind. He does not belong in the category of those who lack 'inwit' and, according to Wit, should justly be supported by others (IX 68–73).

# Index